アカデミック ライティング 入門【第2版】

英語論文作成法

吉田友子
Tomoko Yoshida

慶應義塾大学出版会

アカデミックライティング入門
目　次

学習をはじめる前に　*8*

Part I. Introduction　*11*

1　Overview：総論　*12*

A. Goals for This Book：この本を上手に使うには　*12*
　Comprehension Check 1A　*13*
B. Writing a Research Paper：学術論文とは何だろう　*14*
　Comprehension Check 1B　*20*
　Reading 1B を振り返って　*22*
　♠ レポートという言葉について　*23*
　Writing for Fun: Business Letters　*23*
　英語を学ぶために便利なサイト　*26*

Part II. Planning & Researching　*27*

2　Initial Planning：初めに考えること　*28*

A. Choosing & Narrowing a Topic：良いトピックとは何か　*28*
　Comprehension Check 2A　*29*
　♠ この教科書のトピックがまとまるまで　*30*
　◎ トピックの絞り方　*31*
　Exercise 2A-1: Narrowing Down a Topic　*32*
　Exercise 2A-2: Narrowing Down a Topic　*33*

3

B. **Brainstorming & Mindmapping**：
私の頭の中にはどんなアイディアがあるだろう　*34*

   Comprehension Check 2B　*36*
   Exercise 2B-1: Brainstorming　*39*
   Exercise 2B-2: Mindmapping　*40*
   Exercise 2B-3: Choosing & Narrowing Down a Topic　*41*
   Applications 2B-1: Choosing & Narrowing Down a Topic　*43*
   Exercise 2B-4: Brainstorming/ Mindmapping　*44*
   Applications 2B-2: Brainstorming/ Mindmapping　*46*

C. **Thesis Statements**：私は一番何がいいたいのだろう　*47*

   Useful Expressions 2C: Thesis Statements　*47*
   Exercise 2C-1: Creating a Thesis Statement　*49*
   Exercise 2C-2: Creating a Thesis Statement　*50*
   Applications 2C: Creating a Thesis Statement　*51*
   Writing for Fun 2: Business Email Messages　*51*

3　Planning & Organizing：論文の構成を考える　*56*

A. **Organizing**：論文の構成　*56*

   Exercise 3A-1: Organizing　*60*
   Exercise 3A-2: Organizing　*61*

B. **Outlining**：論文の流れを考える　*62*

   Comprehension Check 3B　*63*
   Exercise 3B-1: Making an Outline　*67*
   Exercise 3B-2: Making an Outline　*68*
   Applications 3B: Making an Outline　*69*
   Writing for Fun 3: Resumes/ Curriculum Vitae (CVs)　*70*

4 Researching: 研究する 75

A. Conducting a Literature Review: 研究者達はどのような研究をしてきたのか 75

Comprehension Check 4A 78

B. Taking Notes: メモをとるには 80

Comprehension Check 4B 83
Quoting 85
Useful Expressions 4B 86
Exercise 4B-1: Paraphrasing & Summarizing 90
Exercise 4B-2: Paraphrasing & Summarizing 90

C. Referencing: 使った文献を明示するには 97

Exercise 4C-1: Referencing 101
Exercise 4C-2: Referencing 102
Exercise 4C-3: Using a Library Search Engine 104
Applications 4C: Researching 105
Writing for Fun 4: Cover Letters 106

Part III. Writing the Research Paper 109

5 Writing the Research Paper: Introduction, Body & Conclusion 論文の三要素 110

A. Introduction: 論文の書き出しについて 112

Exercise 5A-1: Introduction の4つの要素 114

(i) 読み手の興味を引くもの 116

5

Exercise 5A-2: Introduction – (i) 読み手の興味を引くもの　　*117*
　　　Exercise 5A-3: Introduction – (i) 読み手の興味を引くもの　　*118*
　　　Exercise 5A-4: Introduction – (i) 読み手の興味を引くもの　　*119*
　(ii) 論文の意図や重要性を示すのに効果的と思われる背景等の説明　　*120*
　　　Useful Expressions 5A　　*121*
　　　Exercise 5A-5: Introduction - (ii) 論文の意図や重要性を示すのに効果的と思われる背景等の説明　　*121*
　(iii) Thesis statement として表す論文の趣旨　　*122*
　(iv) 論文の構成の説明　　*122*
　　　Exercise 5A-6: (iv) 論文の構成の説明　　*123*
　　　Useful Expressions 5A: Introduction - (iv) 論文の構成の説明　　*123*
　　　Exercise 5A-7: Introduction - (iv) 論文の構成の説明　　*125*
　　　❯ 上級者向けのワンポイント　　*126*
　　　Applications 5A: Introduction　　*126*

B. Conclusion：論文の締めくくりについて　　*127*

　　Useful Expressions 5B　　*128*
　　Exercise 5B-1: Conclusion - (i) 要点のまとめ　　*128*
　　Exercise 5B-2: Conclusion - (i) 要点のまとめ　　*129*
　　Exercise 5B-3: Conclusion のまとめ　　*130*
　　❯ 上級者向けのワンポイント　　*131*

C. Body：論文の本文を効果的に表現するには　　*131*

　　Body　　*131*
　　Paragraph　　*131*
　　Exercise 5C-1: Paragraphs　　*133*
　　Exercise 5C-2: Organizing Paragraphs　　*136*
　　Applications 5C: Writing the Paper　　*138*
　　Writing for Fun 5: TOEFL Writing その1　　*139*

6 Completing the Research Paper：論文を完成させるために *141*

A. Not Getting Discouraged：勇気をもって *141*

◎ヒント１：いつ書くかを決めてそれを必ず守る *142*
◎ヒント２：スケジュールをたてる *143*
◎ヒント３：集中する *144*
◎ヒント４：人とのふれあいを大事にする *145*
◎ヒント５：先入観にとらわれない *145*
◎ヒント６：とにかく書く *146*

B. Proofreading & Revising：見直しと書き直しについて *147*

Academic Paper Checklist *148*
Exercise 6B-1: Shortening Long Sentences *150*
Exercise 6B-2: Eliminating Redundancy and Economizing Words *154*

C. Frequently Made Mistakes：良い英語を書くために *156*

Exercise 6C-1: But, And, So & Because *159*
Exercise 6C-2: Word Choice *161*
Exercise 6C-3: 総合練習 *163*

D. Formatting the Paper：形式を整える *165*

Exercise 6D: Titles *167*
Heading の書き方 *167*
Writing for Fun 6: TOEFL Writing その２ *172*

解答例 *174*

学習をはじめる前に

『アカデミック・ライティング』初版が1998年に出版されてから早17年経っている。そのなかで一番ライティングに影響を及ぼした変化はインターネットの普及ではないかと思う。ライティングの際に役に立つ様々な情報が、今、インターネット経由で簡単にアクセスできる。それを踏まえて、今回の改訂版ではインターネットでアクセスできる情報を多く含めるとともに、過去15年間に様々な読者からいただいた貴重なアドバイスに基づく変更も多々加えた。さらに、論文作成経験者に役立つ情報やテクニックも「上級者向けのワンポイント」として一部紹介している。また、電子媒体の文献の増加に伴い、APAマニュアルも大きく変更されたので、新しいルールについての説明も今回加筆した。

本書は、日本人学習者が、英語で論文が書けるよう導くことを目的としている。特に、ある程度英語の文章を書くことはできるが、論文を書いたことはない、または書いたことはあるがどうも思うように書けなかった、という人を対象にしている。

英語論文の書き方を学ぶには、まず論文とはどういうものかを理解する必要がある。次に、資料の調べ方、構成の決め方など、書くための具体的な skill（技術）を身につけることが大事である。それと同時に、英語で書かれている文章をたくさん読むこと、日頃から日常的なことでもなんでも英語でたくさん書いてみることが大切である。そして何より、実際に英語で論文を書いてみることが重要である。

この観点から、本書は次のような構成となっている。

(a) 論文を書くために必要な具体的な技術を身につける

● Reading & Comprehension Check

各章で論文の準備の各段階や構成の方法について英語と日本語で説明していく。説明が英語の場合は Reading として書かれている。読後にポイントをしっかりと把握できたかどうか確認するために Comprehension Check があ

る。Comprehension Check は Reading の内容が理解できていれば、難しくないはずである。Reading の内容を十分把握し、実際に論文を書く時、役立てて欲しい。

● Exercises

　各章は、それぞれ 2 つ以上のセクションに分かれていて、2A、2B などとされている。論文作成の新しい skill がセクションに出てきた場合、それに関連した練習問題がその都度、出されている。

● Applications

　セクションで学んだことを応用し、実際に論文を書いてみる時に役立つものとして Applications がある。この Applications を次々とこなすことによって論文作成の準備が自然にできるはずである。

(b) 英語で書かれている文章をたくさん読む

> The greatest part of a writer's time is spent reading, in order to write a man will turn over half a library to make one book.
> (Samuel Johnson as cited in Charlton, 1997, p. 31)

　母国語でも良い文章を書くのは大変なことである。実際、文章を書こうという人は本を読むことに多くの時間を費やしている。人の書いた文章を通して、構成の仕方や効果的な表現など、学ぶことは多い。良い論文を書くには、英語で書かれている文章をたくさん読むことが大切である。そのためにも本書では説明の部分もなるべく英語で書いている。このテキストで学習し、実際に英語で論文を書く際には、参考文献として英語で書かれた文献にたくさん目を通し、それらを論文の見本として欲しい。

　今はインターネット経由で英語の文献も簡単に手に入るようになった。下記のサイトを利用すると新聞、雑誌、本、参考書やオンライン図書館にアクセスできるので是非お勧めしたい。

http://www.englishpage.com/readingroom/readingroomintro.html

(c) 英語をたくさん書き、英文に慣れる

● Writing for Fun

英文を書く力をつけるにはやはりたくさん書くことである。日記をつける等、毎日なんらかの形で文章を書く習慣をつけるとよい。文法などにはあまりこだわらず、なるべくたくさん書くことを目的にする。たくさん楽しく書くというテーマでこの Writing for Fun を各章末につけた。これ以外にも、インターネット経由でフェイスブック、ブログ、ツイッター等で英語を使い、いろいろな人々と英語で交流することで、楽しく書く力がつくだろう。

(d) 実際に英語で論文を書いてみる

論文の書き方について読んだり、練習問題をこなすことも大切であるが、一番学習効果が高いのは実際に論文を書くことである。そのためにも、このテキストでは、1本論文を書くことを目的としている。できれば実際に提出しないといけない論文を書いた方がやる気もでるので、授業で提出しなくてはならない論文、もしくは論文コンテストや学術誌に投稿したいと思う論文を書いて欲しい。論文を書くには多大な時間がかかるので、具体的な目標をできる限り作って、成果をぜひどこかで実らせて欲しい。

論文とは限られた専門家が書くものではなく、多くの人が自らの研究から学んだことをなるべく多くの人に読んでもらうために発表するものである。学術誌は、高度に理論的な研究から、実践的で取り組みやすい研究まで、いろいろな分野に分かれている。なるべく論文をたくさん読み、研究しよう。

この改訂版を準備する際に多くの方々から貴重なアイディアやアドバイスをいただいた。特に、改訂版へのアドバイスをたくさん下さった深澤はるか先生、小池浩子先生、日向清人先生、横川（室）真理子先生そして本書の下書きを何度も読み、適切なご意見を下さった大矢玲子先生には、心よりお礼申し上げます。

2014 年 12 月
吉田友子

PART I

Introduction

CHAPTER 1

Overview: 総論

Aims:
1. To understand the goals of this book.
2. To gain a better understanding of what is considered good academic writing in English.

1A Goals for This Book
この本を上手に使うには

 **Reading 1A:**

Goals for This Book

Academic Writing is an advanced level textbook for individuals who wish to refine their writing skills. Through reading passages and completing exercises, you will learn the skills necessary to write a good research paper[1] in English. This book will take you, step-by-step, through the necessary stages involved in writing a well-organized paper.

This textbook consists of three main parts. Part I is an overview of this book and aims to give you a general understanding of what is con-

---

1 research paper - 論文〈詳しい定義は Reading 1B を参照〉

sidered good academic writing in English. Part II discusses the steps involved in preparing to write a research paper. Specifically, Chapter 2 describes the initial planning stages, such as narrowing down a topic, composing a thesis statement and brainstorming. Chapter 3 discusses the final process in the planning stage — organizing and outlining. Chapter 4 then introduces strategies in locating relevant outside sources[2] as well as appropriate ways of citing[3] them. The third and final section of the book covers the three main components of an academic paper while providing advice on how to successfully finish it.

Upon completion of this book, you should not only have a better idea of what is considered good academic writing in English, but will also have the experience of actually writing a research paper in English.

✓ Comprehension Check 1A:

1. What should you gain through reading passages and completing exercises in this book?

2. If you want to get a general idea of what this book is about, which part should you read?

3. Which chapters deal with the steps necessary in preparing to write a paper?

4. Which chapter contains information on how to find relevant materials?

2　outside sources - 文献、出典
3　cite - 引用する

5. What should you learn from Part III of this textbook?

6. What are the two things you are expected to gain upon completion of this book?
a.
b.

Writing a Research Paper
学術論文とは何だろう

Writing a Research Paper

A fallacy of some repute and some duration is the one which assumes that because a student can write an adequate essay in his[4] native language, he can necessarily write an adequate essay in a second language. (Kaplan, 1966, p. 3)

According to Kaplan (1966), many foreign students with advanced English proficiency have been told by their instructors that their papers are "somehow out of focus,"[5] "lack organization," or "lack cohesion."[6] In other words, their papers do not appear "logical" to their instructors. If these same students are able to write "well-organized" and "logical" papers in their native language, it would seem only nat-

---

4 この論文が書かれた頃は漠然と「人」を示す代名詞として he が使われていたが、最近アメリカでは男性代名詞を使うのは避けられている。もっと詳しくは第6章で説明されているが、主に複数形の they 等が使われるケースが多い。
5 out of focus - ピントがずれている
6 lack cohesion - うまく結合していない、考えがバラバラ

14

ural for them to be able to transfer this skill to their second language. This, unfortunately, is not always the case. Some researchers (e.g., Kaplan, 1966; Okabe, 1993) argue that this is because the definition as well as purpose of "logic" and "rhetoric"[7] vary across cultures. On the other hand, some studies have shown that the conventions that govern research articles have become universal. For example, Taylor & Chen (1991) compared Anglo-American and Chinese scientific texts and found that the underlying patterns take "virtually no account of language systems, and little account of either national or disciplinary culture" (p. 332). In our increasingly interdependent world, perhaps the standards that govern "good academic writing" have become universal.[8] However, the fact remains that knowledge of the English language is not enough. To write a "good paper" in English, one must first understand the definition, components and purposes of a research paper. This reading passage will, therefore, begin by presenting a definition of a research paper, followed by a summary of the characteristics of an "effective paper" as presented by Langan (1985).

Definition

According to Roberts (1985) a research paper is a "formal essay in which the author seeks to prove a thesis[9] partly by providing evidence gathered from outside sources" (p. 178). To emphasize the relevance of the thesis statement, researchers often begin by conducting a literature review.[10] To fill in the gaps left by previous articles, researchers conduct their own original research. Although it is important to find enough material to support the thesis, the paper should not simply be a random collection of other people's ideas. The main purpose of a

---

7　rhetoric - 修辞学、レトリック、つまり上手な表現法のこと
8　英語の「世界語」化にともなう最近の傾向として、英語以外の言語で書かれた論文でも、英語論文的な論理展開・レトリックが採用されている場合が多い。
9　thesis - 命題、定立、つまり自分がこれから証明しようとするアイディア〈詳しくは47~54ページを参照〉
10　literature review（または literature search）- 文献調査〈詳しくは75~80ページを参照〉

research paper is to present an original thesis and to prove it through logical argument using concrete support obtained from reliable sources.

Characteristics of an Effective Research Paper

To accomplish the above, Langan (1985) emphasizes the importance of the following four points: "to advance a single point (thesis) and stick to that point, to support the point with specific evidence, to organize and connect the specific evidence, and to write clear, error-free sentences" (p. 63). Let us now examine the above four points in more detail.

Advance a single point (thesis) and stick to that point. The main idea is always expressed at the beginning as a thesis statement. The rest of the paper is then organized to logically support the statement (e.g., A is B because of the following three reasons). The arguments are stated clearly and directly without digressing.[11] Non-native English speakers need to be especially careful since, as mentioned earlier, rhetoric and logic tend to be influenced by culture. What you consider "relevant" might be considered "tangential"[12] by your English instructor. Remember that academics reading papers generally skim through[13] and expect them to follow a predictable pattern. They do not expect to be amused or informed about anything other than the thesis being proposed. When in doubt, have your instructor take a look at your outline[14] or rough draft[15] before writing the first draft.

Support the point with specific evidence. The two excerpts below

---

11 digress - 本題からずれる、脱線する
12 tangential - 本題から脱線している
13 skim through - （本などを）ざっと読む、拾い読みする
14 outline - （論文の構成等の）全体像〈詳しくは第３章を参照〉
15 rough draft - （論文の構成等の）下書き〈詳しくは第６章を参照〉

are trying to make the same point: the increase in the number of returnees.[16] The second quote, however, is much more convincing since it has concrete evidence to support the statement: the source of information and statistics.

- The number of children being educated abroad is increasing every year.
- According to the Ministry of Foreign Affair's 1992 survey, there are an estimated 51,000 Japanese children being educated abroad at present. This is three times that of 1975 when there were an estimated 16,000 (Japan Education Almanac Publication Committee, 1993) .

Locating outside sources, therefore, is essential when writing a research paper. Evidence can be obtained from various sources including books, journals, magazines, and interviews. Going through the published literature to locate relevant material is called a literature review. This helps you understand the topic you are writing about better. Citing a variety of sources, particularly recent ones, also indicates to the reader that you are well-informed on the subject and that your conclusions can be trusted. When choosing which materials to use, two things should be considered. One is whether the information is relevant in supporting the thesis statement. The other is whether the information is from a reliable source. Remember, just because something has been published does not guarantee its reliability.

Organize and connect the specific evidence. Once the literature review has been completed, one must decide how to organize the paper to support the thesis statement in a "logical" manner. Oshima & Hogue (1991) propose four useful patterns in organizing essays, namely: chronological order, logical division, cause & effect, and compari-

---

16 returnee - 帰国子女、帰国生

son & contrast.

(1) Chronological order means that information in the paper is organized according to when things happened, from oldest to newest. This is especially useful when explaining historical events, biographies, scientific or technical processes, and progress within a field of study.

(2) Logical division is useful when covering a relatively broad topic. Logical division means separating the topic into two or more categories. This reading passage, for example, is divided into two main categories: (i) definition of a research paper and (ii) characteristics of an effective paper (which is further divided into four subcategories).

(3) When we want to know why a certain phenomenon or event has occurred the most commonly used format is the cause and effect format. The cause and effect format begins by considering various possible factors that might be responsible for causing the particular phenomenon in question. For example, if one were to examine problems in the current educational system, one might begin by first presenting the problems, then exploring some possible causes and finally examining the relationship between the causes and effects.

(4) Comparison and contrast is frequently used to help illuminate differences. Compare the following two excerpts.

1) Traditional Japanese food is relatively low in calories. A standard meal consisting of rice, miso soup, fish and vegetables is only about 300-500 calories.

2) Traditional Japanese food is relatively low in calories. A standard meal consisting of rice, miso soup, fish and vegetables is only about 300-500 calories. *In sharp contrast is a western style meal of spaghetti and salad which can amount to a total of 800-1000 calories.*

Unless the reader is knowledgeable about calories to begin with, the first excerpt is not enough to make a strong impression. The second excerpt, however, is likely to impress most people since a clear comparison is presented.

Write clear, error-free sentences. Although writing "error-free" sentences may seem unrealistic, it is fairly easy to avoid simple and glaring mistakes.[17] Prior to turning in your paper, always proofread it *at least* twice—once to check the flow of the whole paper to make sure that the arguments are clear and logically organized and a second time to check for spelling and grammar mistakes. These mistakes are especially distracting and unnecessary since most word processing programs nowadays can check for spelling and grammar mistakes.

Conclusion

Writing a paper in a second language is not merely a matter of writing something in one's native language and then translating it. Writing, like other forms of communication, is influenced by culture. What is considered good writing in one culture may not be appreciated in another. Hence, to be able to write a good English paper, it is essential to first understand the purpose as well as the characteristics of an effective research paper.

---

17 glaring mistake - 明らかな間違い

References

Kaplan, R. B. (1966). Cultural thought patterns in intercultural education. *Language Learning: A Journal of Applied Linguistics, 16* (1 & 2), 1-20.

Langan, J. (1985). *College writing skills with readings.* New York, NY: McGraw-Hill Book Company.

Okabe, R. (1993). 日本のレトリック [Japan's rhetoric]. In M. Hashimoto & S. Ishii (Eds.), 日本人のコミュニケーション [*Japanese communication styles*] (pp. 55-81). Tokyo: Kirihara-shoten.

Oshima, A., & Hogue, A. (1991). *Writing academic English* (2nd ed.). Menlo Park, CA: Addisson-Wesley Publishing Company.

Roberts, W. H. (1985). *The writer's companion: A short handbook.* Boston, MA: Little, Brown and Company.

Taylor, G., & Chen, T. (1991). Linguistic, cultural and sub-cultural issues in contrastive discourse analysis: Anglo-American and Chinese scientific texts. *Applied Linguistics, 12,* 319-336.

Comprehension Check 1B:

1. According to Okabe and Kaplan, are logic and rhetoric universal?

2. According to the author, what is the first step in learning how to write a good research paper?

3. What is the main purpose of a research paper?

4. According to Langan (1985), what are the four characteristics of an effective paper?

5. Why does the author say that non-native speakers need to be especially careful about stating their arguments clearly and directly without going off on a tangent?

6. What is a literature review?

7. When conducting a literature review, what are the two criteria for determining whether a particular source should be used or not?

8. What are the four suggested patterns in organizing an essay?

9. If you are planning to write a paper on the historical development of women's rights in Japan, which of the four patterns proposed by Oshima and Hogue would you be likely to use?

10. Why does the author state that spelling mistakes are especially unnecessary?

◎ Reading 1Bを振り返って：

　Reading 1Bでは「学術論文とは何だろう」という題名の英語論文を実際に作成しました。これをA4、5ページ（1250語程度）の英語論文のサンプルとして、論文の内容とともに書き方にも注目して研究してください。みなさんが実際に論文を書く際に、特に注意が必要なのは次の諸点です。

- 各セクションの内容が一目瞭然となるように、見出し、小見出しを使う（詳しくは167〜170ページを参照。）
- 引用文の場合、" "で囲み、ページ数を明記する。
  例：（Langan, 1985, p. 63）
- 長い引用文の場合、文章全体をインデントして書く。
  例：A fallacy of some repute and some duration is that one which assumes that because a student can write an adequate essay in his native language, he can necessarily write an adequate one in a second language. (Kaplan, 1966, p. 3)
- 直接的な引用ではなくても、論文や本などから情報を得た場合には出典を明らかにする（例：Taylor & Chen (1991)）。引用ではない場合は" "は必要ないが、著者の姓と出版年は明記すること（詳しくは86〜89ページを参照。）各パラグラフに複数（3から4）の出典をあげるのが望ましい。
- Referencesには、論文に引用した文献、出典を明記した文献のみを記す。論文を書く際に読んだけれど、本文中に明示しなかったものはReferencesには載せない。表記の仕方は97〜101ページを参照。また、参考文献は著者の姓のアルファベット順に並べる。
- Introductionは、論文のテーマを明確に打ち出すと同時に、論文の構成や、論証の筋道などを読者に提示する、非常に重要なセクションである。Introduction執筆にあたっては、入念な準備と、出来上がった原稿の十分な推敲が必要である。(Introductionの書き方については112〜126ページを参照)。

♠ レポートという言葉について…

一般に日本人の学生がいう「レポート」もアメリカでは (research) paper という。学期末に出すレポートは term paper。以下、幾つか例をあげておく。
- essay - 作文、小論文［文体が自由で、個性的な色彩が強い］
- composition - 作文
- article - 学術誌（journal）等に載っている論文
- Senior Thesis - 卒業論文
- Master's Thesis - 修士論文
- (Doctoral) Dissertation - 博士論文

 Writing for Fun 1: Business Letters

　アメリカには英文レターのスタイルは幾つかあるが、一般的に使われているものをここで紹介しよう。
1. まず右上に自分の住所を書き、その下に日付を書く。
2. 1行空け、左上に相手の名前と住所を書く。
3. さらに1行か2行空けて、相手の名前（Dear Mr. Brown 等）を書く。名前が不明の場合は To Whom it May Concernと書き、その後にコロン（：）をつける。
4. 各 paragraph のはじめはインデントせずに左によせて書く。その分、paragraph と paragraph の間は1行空けることになっている。
5. 最後に自分の名前を書き、その上にペンでサインする。

　ビジネスの文章はなるべく簡潔、かつ丁寧に書くことが大事である。インターネット検索で "business letter sample" もしくは "business letter template" と打ち込めばいろいろ出てくるので是非参照しよう。

1-1-1 Hiyoshi
Kohoku-ku, Yokohama-shi
Kanagawa-ken Japan 211-0003

January 4, 2015

Mr. Martin Mead
Human Resources Department
Mead Consulting
2112 Martin Luther King Street
Oakland, CA 93105

Dear Mr. Martin Mead:

I recently learned about your company's summer internship program. I am currently a third year student at XX University and have been studying marketing in my seminar. I have been very interested in your company, especially after reading an article about your XX project that was featured in the Japan Times. I was, therefore, very excited to hear that your company was looking for summer interns. It would be a true honor to be able to apply to your internship program.

Could you kindly send an application packet as well as other relevant information to the following address?

    Hanako Keio
    1-1-1 Hiyoshi, Kohoku-ku
    Yokohama-shi 211-0003 Japan

Thank you very much in advance for your cooperation! I look forward to hearing from you soon!

Sincerely yours,

Hanako Keio

Hanako Keio

YOUR TURN:

前ページの例にならい、以下の指示に従って、手紙を書いてみよう。（但し、宛名・住所は、いずれも架空のものである。）

#1 - Write to: Mr. Paul Parker, Director of Human Resources, Parker Company, 51 Duke Street, Cambridge MA 00000, USA
Ask for: Application packet and other relevant information for a part-time job

#2 - Write to: Ms. Pauline Abe, Admissions Office, ABC University, 1287 Prospect Street, Honolulu, Hawaii 96815, USA
Ask for: Application packet and other relevant information for a summer intensive English program

英語を学ぶために便利なサイト

　「学習をはじめる前に」にも述べたように、インターネットの普及により、英語学習に関しても便利な情報が簡単に手に入るようになった。役に立つサイトの一覧表を掲載するURLをいくつか紹介するので、ぜひブックマークして有効活用するとよい。（注意：URLはよく変わるので、もし下記のURLが無効になってしまっている場合は"English learning sites"や"ESL sites"等と検索するとよい。）
http://oedb.org/ilibrarian/50_essential_resources_for_esl_students/
http://www.teachthought.com/learning/50-incredibly-useful-links-for-ell-educators/
http://www.powayusd.com/projects/edtechcentralnew/ELL.htm
http://www.usingenglish.com/
http://home.hiroshima-u.ac.jp/flare/EnglishStudySite.html

　上記URLにも紹介されているが、その中からライティングに特化したサイトをいくつか以下に記す。
http://grammar.ccc.commnet.edu/Grammar/
https://owl.english.purdue.edu/
http://www.towson.edu/ows/index.asp

PART

Planning & Researching

CHAPTER 2

Initial Planning:
初めに考えること

Aims:
1. To understand the importance of choosing and narrowing down a topic.
2. To learn how to narrow down a topic.
3. To understand the importance of brainstorming and mindmapping.
4. To learn how to brainstorm and mindmap.
5. To understand what a thesis statement is.
6. To learn how to create a thesis statement.

 ## Choosing & Narrowing a Topic
良いトピックとは何か

Choosing & Narrowing a Topic

When assigned to write a research paper or report, there will be times when you will be given a specific topic to write about. Other times you will be given a variety of topics from which to choose. In many cases, the topic will be broad or vague so it can be tailored to the interests of a diverse group. In such a case, choosing and narrowing down a topic is the most important step you will need to take before writing your paper.

A good topic is one that is specific enough for you to cover within the prescribed amount of space. If your topic is too big, your paper will probably be shallow and uninteresting. Your topic should also be one that you are interested in and knowledgeable about. If you are interested and knowledgeable about your topic, you will be more motivated to write about it, making it more interesting for the audience as well (Shaw, 1984).

Thus, when deciding on your topic, ask yourself the following questions.

1. Is this topic specific enough for me to cover within the given amount of space?
2. What aspect of this topic interests me the most?
3. What aspect of this topic am I knowledgeable about?

Narrowing down a topic not only gives a clear direction to a paper, but also ensures sufficient coverage of the topic within the assigned amount of space.

✓ Comprehension Check 2A:

1. What happens when the topic you choose is too big or general?
   _____

2. What are the three things you need to consider when choosing and narrowing down your topic?
   _____

29

♠ この教科書のトピックがまとまるまで

　筆者はこの本を手がけるにあたって、writing のテキストをつくる、という大きな課題のもとに書き出そうとした。しかしどう考えても 1 冊のテキストで英語の writing の全てを十分に取り上げることは無理だと思い、どう絞っていこうか考え始めた（Reading 2A で紹介した Q.1）。そしてさらに自分に問いかけてみた。

　まず "writing" という大きなトピックの中で自分が何に興味をもっているのか（Q.2）、何について一番詳しいのか（Q.3）等を考えながら下記のリストを書き出した。

- 筆者の専門分野は異文化間コミュニケーションなので、論文の書き方が文化によってどのように影響されるのかに興味をもっている。
- 筆者は学生として、そして研究者として論文等を書いてきたことから、論文の書き方に関してはある程度経験がある。
- 筆者はアメリカで働いていた時にビジネスレターやメモ、企画書やレポート等を書いてきた経験から、business writing に関しても少し興味がある。
- 大学生の英語の論文を多数読んだ結果、基本的な論文の書き方を知らない学生が多いことに気付いた。ただし、ある程度基本をつかみさえすれば素晴しい論文を書くことができる学生もいることを知った。

　大学の授業等で提出する論文の場合は、Q.1 ～ Q.3 を自分に問いかけながら書けば十分であるが、ビジネスレポート、学術論文、この本のように出版を目的としているものの場合は、さらに読み手が何に興味を持っているのかを考える必要がある。そこで大学生、一般社会人が英語の writing の何に興味を持っているか考えてみた。

- 大学生の中には将来会社勤めをする方も多いので、business writing にも興味があるのではないか。

● グローバリゼーションの時代、一般的な社会人も英語論文を書かなければならない機会が多くなるのではないか。

最終的にはテキストの長さや自分の興味や知識等を予想される読み手の興味と照らし合わせた結果、英語論文（academic writing）について書くのが一番適切ではないか、という結論にいたった。もし、筆者がトピックを絞らずに writing という大きなトピックのまま書き出したとしたら永久に仕上がらなかったか、中途半端なまま終わらせることになっただろう。

◎ トピックの絞り方：

Reading 2A で簡単にトピックの絞り方について説明したが、実際にトピックを絞ろうとすると、どう手を着けたらよいのか戸惑うかもしれない。その時にここにあげる7つの要素を頭に入れて取り組むと比較的楽である。7つの要素は Arnaudet & Barrett (1981) が提案した8つの要素を筆者がさらにアレンジしたものである。

例えば International Business という大きなトピックを選んで論文を書くとしよう。このトピックの焦点はどのように絞れるか、7つの要素に沿って考えていく。1つの要素だけではトピックが絞りきれない場合、複数の要素を組み合わせて焦点を決定することになる。

1. Time - いつ？（特定の年、時代など）
   International Businesses in the 21st Century/Post-War Era (time)
2. Place - どこで？（国名、地名、地域、場所など）
   Doing Business in Japan/the USA/Eastern Europe (place)
3. Group - 誰が？（国籍や職業など）
   Doing Business with the Japanese/Koreans/Americans (group)
4. Aspect - 様相（具体的な特徴など）
   ●International Joint Ventures/Marketing/Mergers & Acquisitions
   (aspect)

- Doing Business Effectively/Efficiently/Ethically (aspect) across Cultures
5. Similarities & Differences (S&D) - 類似点や相違点（比較対象等の結果）
    - Similarities (S&D) between Japanese and American Businesses
    - A Comparison of (S&D) Japanese and American Small Businesses
    - Cultural Differences (S&D) in the Business Setting
6. Number - 幾つの？（具体的な数字など）
    Five (number) Successful Multinational Companies in Japan: A Comparative Analysis
7. Cause & Effect (C&E) - 原因と結果（何が何を起こすかなどの相互関係）
    - The Effect (C&E) of the "Big Bang" on the New York Stock Exchange
    - Reasons Behind (C&E) Unsuccessful Joint Ventures
    - Adjustment as the Key to Succeeding (C&E) in Another Culture

Exercise 2A-1:　Narrowing Down a Topic

　上記にならってHigher Education[1] という大きなトピックで論文を書くとして、適当な主題を５つ考えなさい。１つの要素で絞りきれない場合は複数組み合わせてもよい。

1. _____
   _____
   _____
2. _____
   _____
   _____
3. _____
   _____
   _____

1　higher education -（大学、大学院、専門学校など高校卒業後の）高等教育

4. _____

_____

_____

5. _____

_____

_____

Exercise 2A-2: Narrowing Down a Topic

左の欄の general topic を絞ったものが右の欄にあげてある。下線の部分が上記の7つの要素のうちのどれにあてはまるかを（　）に記入しなさい。

1. Communication　　　　● Japanese and American (　　　) Communication Styles: A Comparative Analysis (　　　)

2. Environmental Issues　● Three (　　　) Effective Ways (　　　) to Help Save the Environment (　　　)

3. Education　　　　　　● A Comparison of Universities (　　　) in Three (　　　) Cultures: Japan, Germany & the USA (　　　)

4. Racism　　　　　　　● Is Racism an Issue in Japan (　　　)?

5. Gender Equality　　　● Examining the Glass Ceiling[2] (　　　) in Five (　　　) Japanese Companies (　　　)

6. International Business　● Business Etiquette (　　　) in Korea (　　　)

2　glass ceiling - ガラス天井（管理職への昇進をはばむ目に見えない人種的・性的偏見）

2B Brainstorming & Mindmapping
私の頭の中にはどんなアイディアがあるだろう

 Reading 2B:

Brainstorming & Mindmapping

Once you have chosen and narrowed down your topic, you can start brainstorming. Brainstorming is a technique in which individuals allow themselves to think of as many different ideas as possible without passing judgment on them (Osborn, 2013). Ideas are not to be discarded or laughed at[3] because they seem strange or out of place.[4] Instead, everything is written down and then considered later. This is what makes brainstorming both unique and effective. Too often, we prematurely dismiss ideas simply because they are different without considering the new perspective they might add to our thinking. Brainstorming[5] can be very useful in generating ideas for tasks requiring creativity such as reports, speeches, product development, and campaign slogans (Osborn, 2013). Although originally a group activity, brainstorming can also be done alone.

To brainstorm, first write the topic of your report at the top of a piece of paper. Next, think about the topic and jot down[6] as many words or phrases that you can think of. You can do this in English or Japanese, whichever is easier for you. Do not try to make complete sentences or worry about spelling or grammar as that might interfere with your

---

3 laugh at - ばかにする、あざ笑う
4 out of place - 場違いの
5 Brainstorming は今ではビジネスや大学などで幅広く使われているが Wycoff (1991) によると brainstorming が初めて紹介されたのは1939年、Alex Osborn によってである。
6 jot down - 手早く（簡単に）書き留めておく

train of thought.[7] Do not try to evaluate whether or not your idea is a good one. Simply write everything that you can think of in random order (see Figure 2.1). Although it is best to do your brainstorming in a quiet room where you can concentrate, after the initial brainstorming is done, you might want to carry your brainstorming sheet with you for a few days just in case you come up with interesting ideas on the train, at work, or while doing other activities. Brainstorming with other people can lead to ideas you might not have thought of yourself.

Another method of brainstorming is called mindmapping (see Buzan, 1991; Buzan & Buzan, 1996; Rico, 1983; Wycoff, 1991 for more details). When mindmapping, first write the main topic in the middle of the paper and circle it (see Figures 2.3 & 2.4). For example, in Figure 2.3, I wrote "using movies to teach culture" in the middle of the paper and circled it. Unlike brainstorming where everything is written down in random order, mindmapping begins by first forming some general categories. The categories are drawn as branches coming out of the main topic. In Figure 2.3, there are four main categories (実際に使える映画の例、映画の特徴、様々な外国映画による日本人のステレオタイプ、便利な参考文献) coming out of the central topic. Any examples or subcategories should then branch out of those categories. Since your mindmap is likely to grow in many different directions, it is a good idea to use a large sheet of paper. Initially, you might want to try both brainstorming and mindmapping to see which appeals to you more. You may find that you prefer one method for certain types of activities while the other for other types of activities.

Once you are finished brainstorming, take a look at your brainstorming sheet to see if you notice any patterns. Are you leaning toward one view or another? Do you have more information listed under certain categories compared to others? What is the main thrust[8] of

---

7   train of thought - 考えの流れ
8   main thrust - 要旨、主目的

your paper? Write it down. Circle some main ideas you might want to develop further. Look for some basic categories that you can organize your ideas around and reorganize your brainstorming sheet according to those categories. Finally, cross out those items that do not seem to fit into any of the categories (see Figure 2.2). If you are mindmapping, take note of which categories you expanded more than others.

As a result of brainstorming or mindmapping, you should now have a rough idea of what you will be writing about. In the next section, you will learn how to further refine and reorganize your thoughts through formulating a thesis statement.

✓ Comprehension Check 2B:

1. Name some situations in which it might be useful to brainstorm.

2. What is brainstorming?

3. What makes brainstorming both unique and effective?

4. Why is it important not to pay attention to writing complete sentences, spelling and grammar while brainstorming?

5. How is mindmapping different from brainstorming?

⭐ Figure 2.1: Initial Brainstorming Sheet

筆者がもし Using Movies to Teach Culture というトピックで論文を書くとしたらどういう内容のものにしようか brainstorming してみた結果が下記である。思いついたことを全て書き出したので関連性のなさそうなものも入っている。

```
Using Movies to Teach Culture
・Gung Ho  ・Mr. Baseball  ・Rising Sun  ・やくざ
・男尊女卑   ・エコノミックアニマル   ・スラング
・NAFSA の本  ・ファッション  ・時代を反映する
・現実を誇張する  ・伊丹十三の「たんぽぽ」と「お葬式」
・Ellen Summerfield の本   ・文化摩擦
・文化の特徴を表す  ・現実を表す  ・共感できる
・違う視点から自分の文化を見られる  ・見ていて楽しい
・簡単に貸しビデオ屋から借りられる  ・本音と建て前
・ステレオタイプを強化する  ・集団主義
・生きている文化を観察できる  ・ジェスチャー
```

⭐ Figure 2.2: Sorting through the Brainstorming Sheet

次に Figure 2.1 の brainstorming sheet を見ながら、どういうふうに区分できるかを考えてみた。その結果、4つのカテゴリーを発見した。(1) 実際に使える映画の例、(2) 映画の特徴、(3) 様々な外国映画による日本人のステレオタイプ、(4) 便利な参考文献である。以上のカテゴリーに沿って brainstorming sheet を分類し、関係のないものをここで排除した。

```
Using Movies to Teach Culture
・Gung Ho  ・Mr. Baseball  ・Rising Sun     ┐ 実際に使える
・伊丹十三の「たんぽぽ」と「お葬式」         ┘ 映画の例
```

- 文化摩擦・文化の特徴を表す・現実を表す
- 共感できる・生きている文化を観察できる
- 見ていて楽しい・時代を反映する・現実を誇張する
- 違う視点から自分の文化を見られる
- 簡単に貸しビデオ屋から借りられる
- ステレオタイプを強化する ——— 映画の特徴
- やくざ・男尊女卑・本音と建て前
- エコノミックアニマル・集団主義 ——— 様々な外国映画による日本人のステレオタイプ
- NAFSA の本・Ellen Summerfield の本 ——— 便利な参考文献
- ジェスチャー・ファッション・スラング

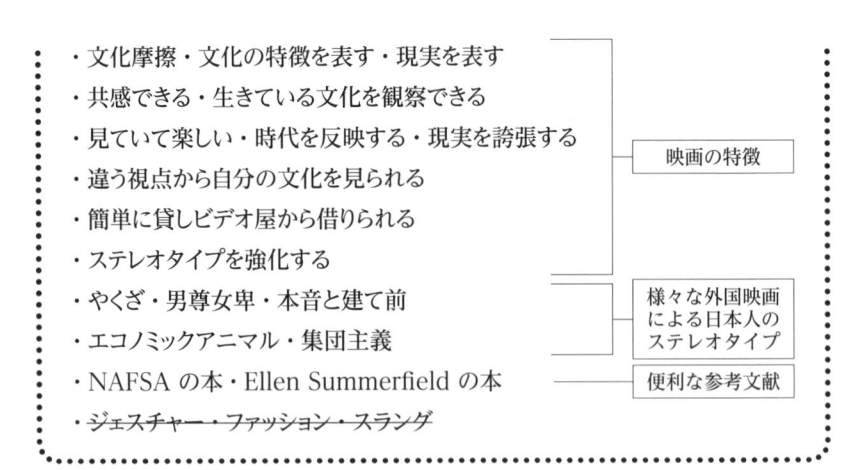

★ Figure 2.3: Mindmapping Sample

　同じトピックで mindmapping をした場合は、あらかじめカテゴリーを考えながら作っていくので、構成の段階に持って行きやすい。

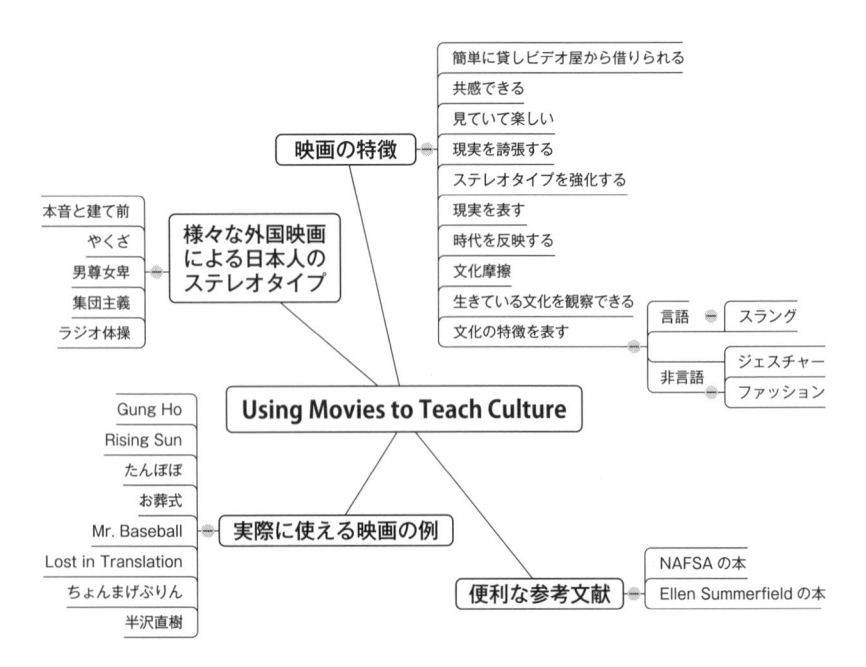

映画の特徴
- 簡単に貸しビデオ屋から借りられる
- 共感できる
- 見ていて楽しい
- 現実を誇張する
- ステレオタイプを強化する
- 現実を表す
- 時代を反映する
- 文化摩擦
- 生きている文化を観察できる
- 文化の特徴を表す
  - 言語 — スラング
  - 非言語 — ジェスチャー / ファッション

様々な外国映画による日本人のステレオタイプ
- 本音と建て前
- やくざ
- 男尊女卑
- 集団主義
- ラジオ体操

Using Movies to Teach Culture

実際に使える映画の例
- Gung Ho
- Rising Sun
- たんぽぽ
- お葬式
- Mr. Baseball
- Lost in Translation
- ちょんまげぷりん
- 半沢直樹

便利な参考文献
- NAFSA の本
- Ellen Summerfield の本

38

⭐ Figure 2.4: Mindmapping of This Textbook

下記は本書を執筆するにあたり作った mindmap である。構想途中のものであるため、最終原稿とは多少異なっている。

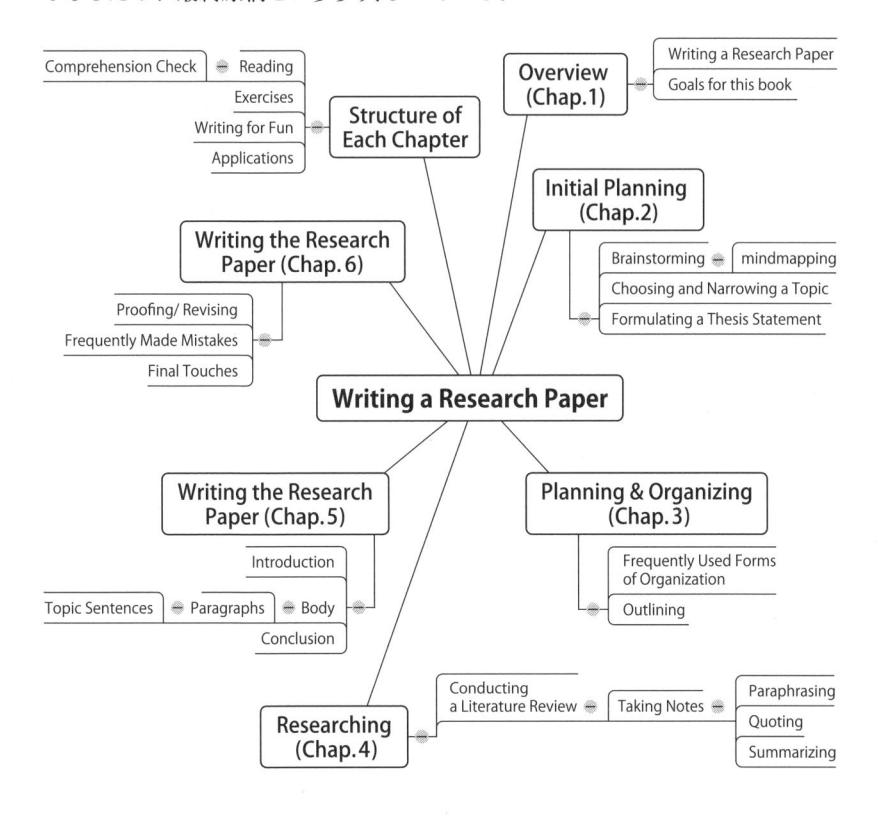

```
Structure of Each Chapter
    ├─ Comprehension Check
    ├─ Reading
    ├─ Exercises
    ├─ Writing for Fun
    └─ Applications

Overview (Chap.1)
    ├─ Writing a Research Paper
    └─ Goals for this book

Initial Planning (Chap.2)
    ├─ Brainstorming ─ mindmapping
    ├─ Choosing and Narrowing a Topic
    └─ Formulating a Thesis Statement

Writing the Research Paper (Chap. 6)
    ├─ Proofing/ Revising
    ├─ Frequently Made Mistakes
    └─ Final Touches

Writing a Research Paper [center]

Writing the Research Paper (Chap. 5)
    ├─ Introduction
    ├─ Paragraphs ─ Topic Sentences
    ├─ Body
    └─ Conclusion

Planning & Organizing (Chap. 3)
    ├─ Frequently Used Forms of Organization
    └─ Outlining

Researching (Chap.4)
    └─ Conducting a Literature Review ─ Taking Notes
            ├─ Paraphrasing
            ├─ Quoting
            └─ Summarizing
```

🔒 Exercise 2B-1:　Brainstorming

まず、brainstorming に慣れるために身近な話題から始めよう。下記のトピックの中から2項目選び、brainstorming しなさい。Brainstorming の方法は Reading 2B を参照すること。スペースが不足なら別紙を用いなさい。

毎月2万円節約する方法／最低限の努力で家の中をきれいにする方法／今現在の仕事の効率を倍にする方法／TOEFL iBTの点数を100点以上にする方法

Brainstorming の結果、何か画期的なアイディアが出てきただろうか。このように、brainstorming 法を日常生活に用いることによって固定観念にとらわれず、新鮮な発想ができるようになる。

🔓 Exercise 2B-2:　Mindmapping

Mindmapping にも慣れるために身近なもので練習するとよい。次の2つのトピックについて、下の例を参照しながら、別紙を用いて mindmapping しなさい。

- イベント（お誕生日会、忘年会、お花見、運動会など）の企画
- 休暇（週末や夏休みなど）の旅行や遊びの計画

Planning a Christmas Party

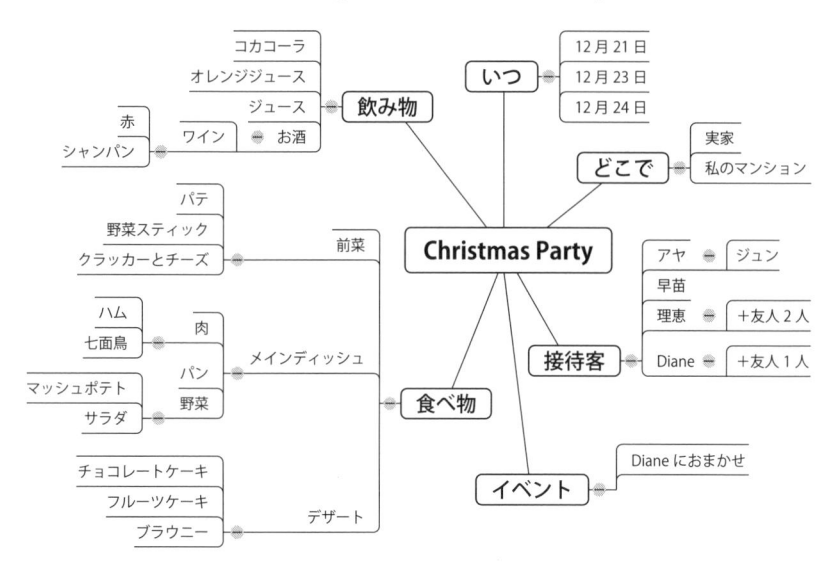

```
                    コカコーラ              12月21日
              オレンジジュース       いつ ── 12月23日
         赤    ジュース                     12月24日
    ──  ワイン ── お酒 ── 飲み物
  シャンパン                                    実家
                                    どこで ──
                                             私のマンション
           パテ
      野菜スティック
   クラッカーとチーズ ── 前菜
                              Christmas Party
                                              アヤ ═ ジュン
      ハム         肉                          早苗
    七面鳥                    接待客 ── 理恵 ═ +友人2人
              メインディッシュ                Diane ═ +友人1人
           パン
   マッシュポテト 野菜
       サラダ                    食べ物
                                              Dianeにおまかせ
                           イベント ──
   チョコレートケーキ
    フルーツケーキ
       ブラウニー ── デザート
```

🔓 Exercise 2B-3: Choosing & Narrowing Down a Topic

　下記のトピックの中から3つを選び、それぞれについて自分が今の時点で知っていること、興味のあることを書き出し（brainstorming）、5枚（1250語程度）のレポートにふさわしい大きさに絞りなさい。

Possible Topics:

Education in Japan	Quality of Life	Japanese Culture
Lifelong Education	Movies	Relationships
Leisure Time Activities	Environment	Food
Doing Business across Cultures		Lifelong Career

■ Example ■

General Topic: Movies
My Interests: I'm interested in culture and cultural differences. Some movies show many interesting cultural characteristics and differences. Movies are fun to watch. I'm always interested in materials I can use in class.
My Knowledge: I know the basic theories in Intercultural Communication. I've seen some books that discuss the use of movies and videos to teach culture. I've attended some seminars and workshops that have effectively used movies and videos to teach culture and cultural differences. I've used movies to teach different aspects of culture.
Specific Topic: Using Movies to Teach Culture

1. General Topic: _____
   Your Interests: _____
   _____
   _____
   _____

   Your Knowledge: _____
   _____
   _____

   Specific Topic: _____
   _____

2. General Topic: _____
   Your Interests: _____
   _____
   _____
   _____

Your Knowledge: _____
_____
Specific Topic: _____
_____
3. General Topic: _____
Your Interests: _____
_____
_____
Your Knowledge: _____
_____
Specific Topic: _____
_____

CHAP 2

Initial Planning

🍎 Applications 2B-1: Choosing & Narrowing Down a Topic

「学習をはじめる前に」で述べた通り、このテキストで勉強する目的は論文を１本書き上げることである。もしすでに授業で課題を与えられているのであれば、それに従って、大きなテーマを絞り、自分の興味、知識をまとめ、Exercise 2A-2 の右の欄にあるように、適当な大きさのトピックを設定しなさい。授業で指定された長さで書けるようなトピックにするように。（ただし、これは現段階での仮のトピックである。 Brainstorming 等の結果、後になってトピックを変えることは問題ない。）もし、学術誌に投稿する場合は自分の興味のある研究テーマを幾つか書き出し、それを絞ってみなさい。

General Topic: _____
Your Interests: _____
_____
_____

43

Your Knowledge: _____
_____
_____
_____
_____

Your Topic: _____
_____

🔓 Exercise 2B-4:　Brainstorming/Mindmapping

　まず Exercise 2B-3 で絞った３つのトピックを下欄にそれぞれ記入しなさい。次に指定された長さのレポートを書くと仮定し、どのような内容にするかなどを brainstorming 法か mindmapping 法を用いて、その下のスペースに記入しなさい。その際なるべく視野を広く持ち、一見とっぴで関連性がなさそうな事柄でも必ず書くようにしなさい。 Brainstorming をする場合、一通り書き終えたものをもう一度見ながら関連性のあるもの同士でカテゴリーを作ったり、使えなさそうなものを省いたりしなさい。スペースが不足なら別紙を用いなさい。

1. Specific Topic: _____

2. Specific Topic: _____

3. Specific Topic: _____

CHAP 2

Initial Planning

Applications 2B-2: Brainstorming/Mindmapping

　この段階から、書こうと思う論文の内容について考え始めなさい。まずは Applications 2B-1 で絞ったトピックを下欄に記入し、その下のスペースまたは別紙にて brainstorming または mindmapping を行いなさい。基本的には紙とペンさえあればことは足りるが、最近は mindmapping 用のコンピュータ・ソフトウェアも多数あるので、試してみる価値はある。ソフトを使ったほうが、書き直しや移動が簡単にできてよいと感じるかもしれない。逆にペンで書いたほうがどこでもできて便利だと感じるかもしれない。自分にとって一番やりやすい形をぜひ見つけて欲しい。ソフトウェアはインターネットの検索で mindmapping tool と検索すれば色々出てくる。ちなみに、この章の mindmap のサンプルは Xmind 2013　http://www.xmind.net/download/win/ というソフトを使用した。

Your Topic:_____

2C Thesis Statements
私は一番何がいいたいのだろう

　トピックを絞り、brainstormingをした結果、だいたい何について書くか決まったら、thesis statementを考えよう。Thesis statement（命題）とは論文の方向性を表わすsentenceのことである。そこでは「この論文では日本の会社における雇用機会均等法について検討します」等といった漠然としたテーマを紹介するのではなく、「1985年に雇用機会均等法が成立したにもかかわらず、多くの日本の会社ではいまだに何らかの形で男女の差別が存在している」等とはっきりとした意見、論証の目的または方向性を示すことが大切である（Langan, 1985）。そして、論文ではそのthesis statementを検証することを目的とするので、なるべくその目的からそれずに、論文を書きながら繰り返しthesis statementを頭に思いうかべるとよい。

　Thesis statementを作成する際には、幾つかの方向性を持つのではなく、1つの限られた方向性を持つことが大事である。また、書こうとする論文の長さ等を考えながら限られた分量で検証できそうなthesis statementにすることも肝心である。Thesis statementをどこに置くかは人それぞれであるが、多くの場合、introductionの最後の方に書かれている。

Useful Expressions 2C: Thesis Statements

　"Useful Expressions"では便利な表現を幾つか紹介する。英語論文でよく使われる表現を網羅的に紹介しているものとしては崎村耕二（1991）の『英語論文によく使う表現』（創元社）がある。ただし、分野によって用いるスタイルや専門用語が違ううえに、学術誌によってもそれぞれの特徴がある。上記の本や次ページのリストを参照する他にも、自分の分野の論文等を多数集めて、どのような表現が使われているかを目的別にリストアップすることをお勧めする。（下線の部分を入れ替えながら独自の文章を作成していくとよい。）

- The number of companies outsourcing their training is increasing/decreasing because of the ongoing recession.
- The Internet is changing our communication patterns in three important areas: personal correspondence, business correspondence and information sharing.
- Choosing a career that one can continue for life is becoming more important in today's world because of the continued rise in people's life expectancy.
- An effective resume should be both concise and informative.
- Company X's failure to succeed in Japan can be traced to the following causes: failure to adapt their products to the Japanese market, insufficient knowledge of Japanese business practices, and Japan's closed market.
- This study investigates how the westernization of the Japanese diet has affected the physique of the Japanese people.
- The purpose of this study was to determine the effect of leisure time activities on stress.
- Offering Kentucky Fried Chicken as a prototype, this paper addressed the issue of adjusting management styles to the host culture.
- This study was designed to determine the effects of class size on language acquisition.
- For improved quality of life to occur, Japanese corporations need to change their policy on overtime work and paid vacations.

Exercise 2C-1: Creating a Thesis Statement

次の 1～5 のトピックを読み、それぞれにふさわしい thesis statement を a～e から選びなさい。

( ) 1. A Bribe or a Gift : Ethics in Doing Business Internationally
( ) 2. Examining the Glass Ceiling in Five Japanese Companies
( ) 3. Apologies in Japan
( ) 4. Should Age be an Issue When Entering a University?
( ) 5. Effective Recycling: What Needs to be Done?

---

a. For effective recycling to occur, consumers need to actively purchase recycled goods.

b. Since people learn the most when they want to learn, motivation should be the criteria for entering a university, not age.

c. When doing business across cultures, one may find a "perfectly appropriate gift" mistaken for a bribe.

d. Since human relationships are of utmost importance to many Japanese, apologies serve an important purpose in Japanese society.

e. Although Equal Employment Opportunity (E.E.O.) is required in Japanese companies, most places have invisible barriers that block women from being promoted to executive level positions.

Exercise 2C-2: Creating a Thesis Statement

ここで Exercise 2B-3 (41～43ページ) で選んだ general topic とそれを絞った結果できた specific topic を下の解答欄に記入し、Exercise 2B-4 (44～45ページ) で行った brainstorming か mindmapping の結果をみながら、次の3つのポイントに沿って、thesis statement を作成しなさい。

Guidelines for Creating a Thesis Statement
1. 漠然とテーマを紹介するのではなく、はっきりとした意見、目的、または方向性を示す。
2. 論文の長さ等を考えながら、限られた分量で検証できそうな thesis statement にする。
3. Thesis statement は、幾つもの方向性を持つのではなく、1つの限られた方向性を持つことが大事である。

1. General Topic:＿＿＿＿＿＿＿＿＿＿＿＿＿＿＿＿＿＿＿＿＿＿
   Specific Topic:＿＿＿＿＿＿＿＿＿＿＿＿＿＿＿＿＿＿＿＿＿＿
   Thesis Statement:＿＿＿＿＿＿＿＿＿＿＿＿＿＿＿＿＿＿＿＿
   ＿＿＿＿＿＿＿＿＿＿＿＿＿＿＿＿＿＿＿＿＿＿＿＿＿＿＿＿＿
   ＿＿＿＿＿＿＿＿＿＿＿＿＿＿＿＿＿＿＿＿＿＿＿＿＿＿＿＿＿

2. General Topic:＿＿＿＿＿＿＿＿＿＿＿＿＿＿＿＿＿＿＿＿＿＿
   Specific Topic:＿＿＿＿＿＿＿＿＿＿＿＿＿＿＿＿＿＿＿＿＿＿
   Thesis Statement:＿＿＿＿＿＿＿＿＿＿＿＿＿＿＿＿＿＿＿＿
   ＿＿＿＿＿＿＿＿＿＿＿＿＿＿＿＿＿＿＿＿＿＿＿＿＿＿＿＿＿
   ＿＿＿＿＿＿＿＿＿＿＿＿＿＿＿＿＿＿＿＿＿＿＿＿＿＿＿＿＿

3. General Topic:＿＿＿＿＿＿＿＿＿＿＿＿＿＿＿＿＿＿＿＿＿＿
   Specific Topic:＿＿＿＿＿＿＿＿＿＿＿＿＿＿＿＿＿＿＿＿＿＿
   Thesis Statement:＿＿＿＿＿＿＿＿＿＿＿＿＿＿＿＿＿＿＿＿
   ＿＿＿＿＿＿＿＿＿＿＿＿＿＿＿＿＿＿＿＿＿＿＿＿＿＿＿＿＿
   ＿＿＿＿＿＿＿＿＿＿＿＿＿＿＿＿＿＿＿＿＿＿＿＿＿＿＿＿＿

Applications 2C: Creating a Thesis Statement

ここで Applications 2B-2 (46ページ) で作成した brainstorming または mindmapping の結果を参照しながら書こうと思う論文のための thesis statementを作成しなさい。論文作成の過程で、文献調査が進み自らの考えが深まるにつれ、変更、訂正されることも当然ありえる。あくまでも仮のthesis statement として考えるとよい。

Writing for Fun 2: Business Email Messages

日本語のメールと同様、英語のビジネスメールは紙媒体の手紙ほど形式にこだわらなくてもよい。ここでいくつか簡単なポイントを紹介しよう。インターネットでも様々な例文やアドバイスが手に入るので "business email how to" で検索してみよう。

To: ←相手のメールアドレスを書く
Subject: ←用件を書く
cc: ←Carbon copyの略である。上司や部下、チームメンバーなど要件を把握しないといけない人のメールアドレスを書く。パソコンが普及する前はカーボン用紙を使って複写していたため、今でもcc:と呼ばれている。ここのメールアドレスは全員に見えてしまう。
bcc:←Blind carbon copyの略である。cc:の相手の名前やメールアドレスが

見えてほしくない場合はbcc:を使う。
ワンポイントアドバイス：要件はなるべく簡潔に書く。短いパラグラフ（3-4 sentence位のもの）が望ましい。ただし、1 sentenceごとの改行は避ける。

では、ここで下記の内容のメールを下記の相手に書いてみよう。
内容：先週初めてお目にかかった商談相手のMs. Smith。前回のお礼と次回の打ち合わせの日程を決める。
相手のメールアドレス：smith@example.com
cc：自分の上司のメールアドレス (boss@example.com)

To: smith@example.com
cc: my.boss@example.com
Subject: Thank you and setting up our next appointment

Dear Mr. Smith,
cc: my.boss

Thank you so much for taking time out of your busy schedule to meet with me last week. I really enjoyed our conversation and am looking forward to discussing some new ideas again soon. Would it be possible to meet again next week?

I am available on the following dates and times: August 5th (10:00 am to 12:00 noon), 6th (2:00-5:00 pm), 8th (any time). Please let me know when and where is most convenient for you. Thank you once again and I look forward to hearing from you soon!

Sincerely,
Tomoko

****
Tomoko Yoshida
Professor, Faculty of Business & Commerce
Keio University, 4-1-1 Hiyoshi
Kohoku-ku, Yokohama-shi, Kanagawa-ken 223-8521
Tel:###-###-####
Fax: ###-###-###
Email: tomokoyoshida@example.com
Web site: http://tomokoyoshida.example-com

YOUR TURN :

　上記の例にならって、次の要領でメールを書いてみよう。(但し、宛名・住所は、いずれも架空のものである。) メールを書くにあたり、cc:またはbcc:をする必要があるかも検討するように。

Situation 1: You just had a meeting with your client, Mr. Paul Purdy. Your boss, Ms. Janet Jones, also attended this meeting with you. You were in charge of taking minutes for the meeting. Please send the minutes to Mr. Paul Purdy. Please consider whether or not to "cc:" or "bcc:" your boss, Ms. Janet Jones.
Write to: Mr. Paul Purdy <purdy@purdy.com>, your boss is Ms. Janet Jones <jones@jones.com>

Situation 2: Your professor, Dr. Tomoko Yoshida, has just introduced you to a friend, Ms. Sharon Svenson, who is looking for someone to work at her company part-time in her marketing department. Please write Ms. Svenson asking her about this potential position. Again, consider whether or not to cc: or bcc: Dr. Yoshida.

Write to: Ms. Svenson <svenson@svenson.com>, your professor is Dr. Tomoko Yoshida <yoshida@yoshidauniversity.ac.jp>

References

Arnaudet, M. L., & Barrett, M. E. (1981). *Paragraph development: A guide for students of English as a second language.* Englewood Cliffs, NJ: Prentice Hall.

Buzan, T. (1991). *Use both sides of your brain* (3rd ed.). New York, NY: E. P. Dutton.

Buzan, T., & Buzan, B. (1996). *The mind map book: How to use radiant thinking to maximize your brain's untapped potential.* New York, NY: Plume.

Langan, J. (1985). *College writing skills with readings.* New York, NY: McGraw-Hill Book Company.

Osborn, A.F. (2013). *Brainstorming: The Dynamic Way to Creative Ideas* [Unabridged] [Audible Audio Edition]. M-y Books Ltd.

Rico, G. L. (1983). *Writing the natural way: Using right brain techniques to release your expressive powers.* New York, NY: J. P. Tarcher.

Shaw, H. (1984). *A complete course in freshman English* (8th ed., alternate version). New York, NY: Harper & Row.

Wycoff, J. (1991). *Mindmapping: Your personal guide to exploring creativity and problem-solving.* New York, NY: Berkeley Books.

CHAPTER 3

Planning & Organizing:
論文の構成を考える

Aims:
1. To understand better some commonly used methods of organizing a research paper.
2. To understand how to make an outline.

3A Organizing
論文の構成

　Brainstorming や mindmapping の結果、論文のおおまかな構成が決まり、thesis statement を作成したことにより、論旨がより明確になったはずである。ここでは論文をより論理的なものにするために構成の仕方や手順について述べていきたい。

　まず、専門分野によってある程度論文の構成が決まっている場合がある。例えば、心理学や社会学等で実験や調査報告をする場合は次ページの Figure 3.1 のような構成で書かれることが多い。まずは、Introduction で問題の定義や重要性の説明から始め、次に Literature Review で先行研究を紹介する。Methods では用いた研究方法について詳しく述べ、Results で研究の結果を報告する。さらに、Discussion で研究の結果をわかりやすく説明し、Conclusion で結論を述べ、今後の研究の展開などの提案をする。

★ Figure 3.1

> Introduction（問題の定義等）
> Literature Review（先行研究の紹介）
> Methods（研究で用いた方法の詳説）
> Results（研究のデータ等の報告）
> Discussion（研究結果についての解説）
> Conclusion（まとめ）

　あらかじめ使う構成が決まっていない場合はReading 1Bで紹介したように、大きく分けて論文の本文の構成の形式は4通りある、と考えてよい(Oshima & Hogue, 1991)。ここではOshima & Hogueの4つをさらにわかりやすくし、5つのパターンとして紹介する。

Chronological Order（年代順）
　年代順に説明する。歴史的背景の説明などに便利である。
Sequential Order（順序をたどる）
　手順や工程の説明などに便利である。
Logical Division（カテゴリー別）
　内容を幾つかのカテゴリーに分け、カテゴリー別に説明する。一番応用範囲が広いため、ほとんどのトピックに用いることができる。
Cause & Effect（原因と結果）
　原因と結果を分けて説明する。特定の現象を起こす原因などを推測する場合などに使う。
Comparison & Contrast（比較対照）
　2つ以上のものを比較して違いを明らかにする。例えば文化の比較や小説に出てくる登場人物の比較、経営システムの比較等と応用範囲は広い。

トピックによってはそれにふさわしい構成が自然と決まることもある。そうでない場合は、構成法を変えることで、同じトピックでも様々なアプローチの仕方があって面白い。例えば下記の5つのトピックで論文を書くとしたらどのようなアプローチが適当かを考えてみよう。ここにも幾つか例を挙げているが、これ以外にも色々な方法がある。ここでは単独の形式をとるものとして説明しているが、長い論文では幾つかのパターンを組み合わせて書くこともある。

a. A Bribe or a Gift: Ethics in Doing Business Internationally

　国によって贈り物と賄賂の定義が異なるため、国際的にビジネスを展開する場合、様々な問題が起こりうる。論文の構成の仕方によってどこに焦点をあてていくかが自然と決まってくる。例えば、comparison & contrast を用い、いくつかの国をとりあげ、接待や贈り物に対しての慣習を比較するのであれば、ビジネス文化の違いが焦点となる。また、chronological division を用い、国際的に話題を呼んだ事件や法律の導入などを年代順に紹介していく場合は、文化と国際問題の変容が焦点となる。また、logical division を用い、接待や贈り物に関しての文化摩擦のケース・スタディをいくつか紹介し、分析していく場合はそれぞれのケースの特徴が議論の主体となる。

b. Examining the Glass Ceiling in Five Japanese Companies

　この title でもわかるように、論文の内容は5つの会社におけるグラス・シーリングの比較である。ただ、comparison & contrast をするにもいろいろな方法がある。例えば chronological order を用い、5つの会社の過去15年間のグラス・シーリングの歴史を追いながら比較していく場合、社会全体の潮流が見えてくる。また、logical division を用い、5つの会社のグラス・シーリングを幾つかのカテゴリー別に比較していくのであれば、グラス・シーリングの多様なあり方が分かってくる。また、cause & effect を用い、5つの会社におけるグラス・シーリングの原因と結果を比較する場合、女性がどのようにグラス・シーリングによって見えない差別を経験しているかの実情が明らかになる。

c. Japanese Styles of Apology

　日本式の謝り方について論ずる場合も、構成によって全く違う論文になる。例えば、logical division を使って謝り方をいくつかの分類にすることができる。軽度な過ちの場合から重度の過ちの場合まで、数段階の過ちの謝り方を解説する場合、日本式の謝り方のハウツーを説明することになる。また、comparison & contrast を用い、違う国の謝り方と比較する場合、他国との比較により、日本独特な傾向が明らかになる。または、cause & effect を用い、日本に焦点をあてながらなぜ日本人は自分の責任でなくても謝るかについての原因（島国である日本では人間関係が重要）と結果（謝ることによって人間関係を円滑にする）を分析することで日本文化全体の理解にもつながっていく。

d. Should Age be an Issue When Entering a University?

　日本ではほとんどの人は高校を卒業した直後または１－２年後に大学に入学するが、国によっては子育てが終わり、一段落した40代の女性や定年退職した方が大学に通うのも珍しくない。大学に入学する時の年齢について論文を書く場合にもやはり構成によって議論のポイントが変わってくる。例えば comparison & contrast で日本対アメリカの比較にすれば、両国の文化の差が見えてくる。同じ comparison & contrast でも18歳で入学する場合と40代で入学する場合の長短所の比較をすることも出来る。または、logical division を使って大学の目的、大学として社会人入学者を受け入れるメリット、デメリットについて書くこともできる。

e. Recycling in Tokyo: Behind the Scenes

　東京のリサイクル事情という漠然としたテーマなので、構成の仕方でいろいろな論文が書ける。例えば、comparison & contrast を用い、理想的なリサイクルの過程と現在東京で行われているリサイクルの状況を比較することによって東京の現状がどのくらい理想に近いかが分かる。Sequential order を用いてゴミが捨てられるところから順にリサイクルの

過程を説明することによって、東京ではどのようにゴミがリサイクルされてきているかを明らかにすることもできる。Logical division を用い、カテゴリー別にリサイクルの状況の説明をすることによってゴミの種類のリサイクル状況（例：アルミ、紙、ペットボトル）を分析したり、cause & effect を用いて、自分の関心のあるゴミ問題の原因を探ることもできる。

🔓 Exercise 3A-1:　Organizing

下記のトピックについて論文を書くとしたらの5つのパターン（chronological order, sequential order, logical division, cause & effect, comparison & contrast）のうちどれが適当か考えなさい。複数のパターンが該当するトピックもあるので注意すること。

1. How to Exchange Business Cards in Japan ＿＿＿＿＿＿＿＿
2. Gift Giving in Three Cultures ＿＿＿＿＿＿＿＿＿＿＿＿＿＿
3. A Brief History of the U.S.-Japan Trade Friction ＿＿＿＿＿
4. What Prompts Juvenile Delinquency? ＿＿＿＿＿＿＿＿＿＿
5. Japanese and American Communication Styles＿＿＿＿＿＿
6. Preventing Cancer ＿＿＿＿＿＿＿＿＿＿＿＿＿＿＿＿＿＿＿
7. 101 Ways to Avoid Writer's Block ＿＿＿＿＿＿＿＿＿＿＿＿
8. The Life and Works of Yukichi Fukuzawa ＿＿＿＿＿＿＿＿
9. The Women's Liberation Movement in Japan: A Brief History ＿＿＿＿＿＿＿＿＿＿＿＿＿＿＿＿
10. Integrating Email into the English Classroom ＿＿＿＿＿＿

Exercise 3A-2: Organizing

Exercise 2B-3（41ページ～）で絞ったトピックをまず下欄に記入しなさい。次にExercise 2B-4（44ページ～）の brainstorming または mindmapping の結果と 2C-2（50ページ）で作成した thesis statement を記入し、それらを参照しながら、どのように構成していくかを簡潔に記しなさい。

1. Specific Topic:
   Thesis Statement:
   Organization:

2. Specific Topic:
   Thesis Statement:
   Organization:

3. Specific Topic:
   Thesis Statement:
   Organization:

3B Outlining
論文の流れを考える

Reading 3B:

Outlining

When painting a picture, most artists start by making a rough sketch in pencil or charcoal. The sketch is then looked at and revised until the artist is happy with it. It is at this point that the artist starts to use paint to add color and texture. An outline is much like the sketch that the artist makes. By making an outline, the writer puts on paper a "sketch" of the main points and ideas and can then look at the whole picture to decide what, if any, changes are necessary. In the same way that sketching a picture before painting not only saves a significant amount of time and effort, but often leads to a higher quality painting, many writers find outlining an essential tool to writing well.[1]

Making an outline based on your brainstorming sheet or mindmap is fairly easy. It is simply a matter of reorganizing and refining your brainstorming sheet or mindmap further. Let us take the revised brainstorming sheet introduced in Chapter 2 (Figure 2.2). Since the main point (Using Movies to Teach Culture) as well as the subcategories (実際に使える映画の例、映画の特徴、様々な外国映画による日本人のステレオタイプ、便利な参考文献) have been decided, it is merely a matter of re-organizing it into outline form (see Figures 3.2 & 3.3).

Once the outline is made, the writer should have a general idea of what the final paper will be like. Here, the following questions should be asked. Is the main point clear? Are the supporting arguments, data

---

1 Like any tool, however, its effectiveness depends on the individual using it. While many writers find outlines indispensable, some prefer the freedom of writing spontaneously without an outline.

or examples convincing? Can everything be covered within the available amount of space? Is there anything that should be included or omitted?

The main advantage to making an outline is that one can examine the paper as a whole to see whether the arguments are clear and logical before actually writing it. Since adjustments can be made before time and effort has been put into shaping the ideas into coherent sentences and paragraphs, outlines can help writers make effective use of their time.

✓ Comprehension Check 3B:

1. What is the main point the first paragraph is trying to make? Please circle one.
   a) When painting, most artists make a rough sketch before actually using paint.
   b) A painting is not complete without paint.
   c) An outline for a writer can be as important as the sketch is for an artist.
   d) It is impossible to write a well-organized paper without an outline.
2. The passage states that making an outline can save time and effort. Please explain.

3. When writing a report, is it absolutely necessary to make an outline?

4. After drafting an outline, what are some questions you should ask yourself?

☆ Figure 3.2: Format of a Simple Outline

　下記に示したのは一番単純な outline の形である。まず、thesis を冒頭で紹介し、それを論証するために必要な理由や説明や資料を1つずつ取り上げていく。最後に conclusion でもう一度 thesis を主張する。

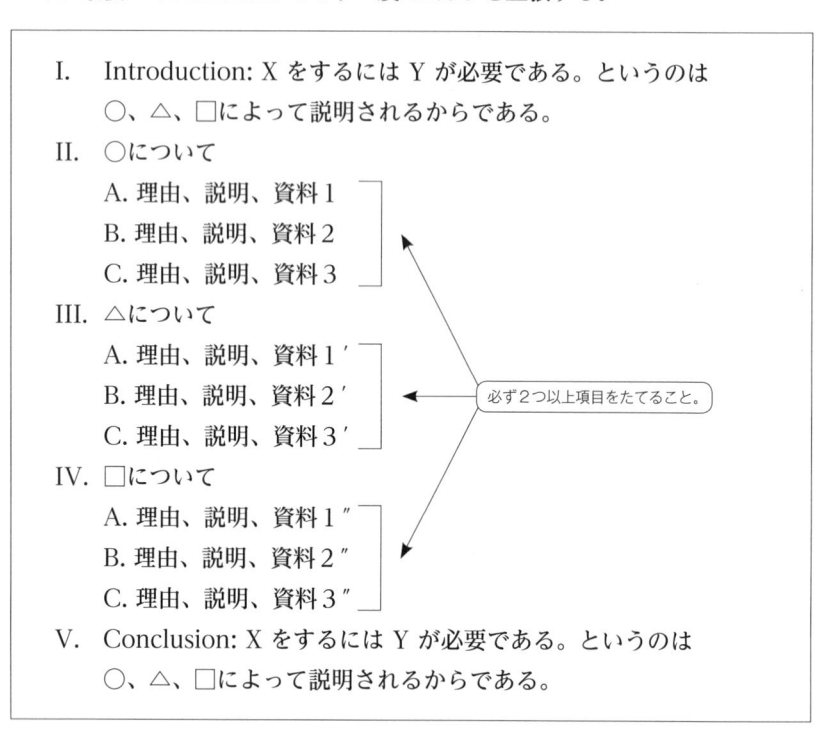

```
I.   Introduction: X をするには Y が必要である。というのは
     ○、△、□によって説明されるからである。
II.  ○について
     A. 理由、説明、資料 1  ┐
     B. 理由、説明、資料 2  │
     C. 理由、説明、資料 3  ┘
III. △について
     A. 理由、説明、資料 1′ ┐
     B. 理由、説明、資料 2′ │ ← 必ず2つ以上項目をたてること。
     C. 理由、説明、資料 3′ ┘
IV.  □について
     A. 理由、説明、資料 1″ ┐
     B. 理由、説明、資料 2″ │
     C. 理由、説明、資料 3″ ┘
V.   Conclusion: X をするには Y が必要である。というのは
     ○、△、□によって説明されるからである。
```

☆ Figure 3.3: Sample Outline

　Brainstorming や mindmapping の結果、構成がだいたい決まったら、それに沿って outline を書くのは簡単である。下記は Figure 2.1 と 2.2 の brainstorming sheet、そして 2.3 の mindmap（37〜38ページ）をもとに書いた outline の一例である。

Using Movies to Teach Culture

I. Thesis: 映画は自国の文化を見つめ直すのに効果的な手段として使える。

II. 映画を使うことによる利点：文化とはその人にまとわりついている、まるで空気のようなものだけに、自国の文化をはっきり認識するのは難しい。そこで自国の文化と他国の文化を比較してその相違点を発見することで、自国の文化を知るという方法がよく使われる。その手段の1つとして、自国の人や物をテーマに取り上げた他国の映画からの学習がある。映画は何でも大げさにし、ステレオタイプをさらに誇張する傾向があるので、これをあらゆる視点から分析することによって今まで気付かなかった自国の文化を発見することができる。

III. 授業の進め方

> 必ず2つ以上項目をたてること。最低でもA、Bは欲しい。

　A. いろいろな映画から短めの場面（3〜5分間位のもの）を集めたものを見せて、簡単なディスカッションを行う。
　B. 一通り見終わった時点で、様々な映画の中で自国の文化がどのように描かれているかを感じたままに絵に描き表し、それを説明してみる。
　C. さらに、次の段階として自国の文化をより正確に表すと思われる絵を直感的に描き、それを説明する。
　D. 自分の文化の中でステレオタイプとは何か？　また、それがどの様な影響を文化に与えているのか？　などをディスカッションする。

IV. 日本文化のステレオタイプを見せるのに効果的な映画
　A. Mr. Baseball

> 必ず2つ以上項目をたてること。最低でも1、2は欲しい。

　　1. 初めの記者会見の場面：本音と建て前の使い分け方など
　　2. 初めの練習の場面：集団行動、和の大切さなど

- B. Rising Sun
    1. 冒頭の場面：バーでカラオケを歌っている場面
        a. 日本といえばやくざ？
        b. 男尊女卑

    〔必ず2つ以上項目をたてること。最低でもA、Bは欲しい。〕

    2. 初めの交渉の場面
        a. 日本人は金もうけのためだったら何でもする
        b. 仕事人間（午前6時半にミーティングを開く）
        c. きちんとしていて清潔好き
    3. パーティーの場面：伝統的なものとモダーンなものがミックスしている
        a. 和太鼓
        b. 着物を着ている女性
        c. 最新の技術を使ったモダーンな建物
- C. Gung Ho
    1. ラジオ体操の場面
        a. 日本人は集団のため、会社のために生きている
        b. ビジネスマンのステレオタイプ：黒いスーツを着てめがねをかけている
    2. 伝統的なものとモダーンなものがミックスしている
        a. 最新の技術を用いて車を製造している
        b. 精神の向上のためにお寺で修行したり、ふんどしをして冷たい川に入ったりしている

V. Conclusion: 映画を用いることは、1つの国の国民性としてあらわれるステレオタイプについての討論を効果的に進める良い方法である。

VI. 付録

〔付録とは論文の本文には入れるには長すぎる又は細かすぎるが読者にとってあると便利な情報を付録A、付録B等と最後に載せる。例えば社会科学の分野の場合、研究で用いたアンケート等を載せる場合が多い。〕

付録 A. 文化を教える場合、便利な文献や映画
   1.   2.

〔この論文を読み、是非映画を使って文化を教えたい方のために参考になる本や映画を箇条書きでリストアップする。〕

付録 B. 授業で学生が実際に描いた絵

〔ここでは授業で学生が実際に書いた絵を幾つかサンプルとして載せる。〕

Exercise 3B-1: Making an Outline

Reading 2B（34ページ～）と 3B（62ページ～）をもう一度読み、これらの文章がどのような outline に沿って書かれたかを下記の例を参照して、推測しなさい。（注：Reading passage は論文としてではなく解説として書かれているので、方向性を持った thesis ではなく一番伝えたいメッセージ、すなわち main idea がある。Reading passage を分析する場合には、main idea を探すように。）

例：

Reading 1B: Writing a Research Paper

I. Introduction - Thesis: To write a "good paper" in English, one must understand the definition, components and purposes of an English "research paper."

II. Definition of a research paper

III. Characteristics of an effective research paper
   A. Advance a single point (thesis) and stick to that point.
   B. Support the point with specific evidence.
   C. Organize and connect the specific evidence.
   D. Write clear, error-free sentences.

IV. Conclusion

Reading 2B: Brainstorming & Mindmapping

I. Introduction - Main idea: _____

_____

II. How to brainstorm:
   A. _____
   B. Think about the topic and jot down as many words or phrases you can think of.

　　　　1. _____
　　　　2. Don't try to make complete sentences; don't worry about spelling or grammar.
　　　　3. Don't evaluate if it is good or not.
　　　　4. _____
　　　　5. _____
　　　　6. _____
　　III. Another method of brainstorming is mindmapping.
　　IV. _____
　　V. Conclusion - As a result of brainstorming or mindmapping, you should now have a rough idea of what you will be writing about.

Reading 3B: Outlining

I. Introduction - Main idea: _____
_____
II. _____
III. _____
IV. Conclusion - The main advantage to making an outline is that one can examine the paper as a whole to see whether the arguments are clear and logical before actually writing it.

🔓 Exercise 3B-2: Making an Outline

　Exercise 2B-4（44 ～ 45 ページ）で作った brainstorming sheet または mindmap と、Exercise 2C-2（50 ページ）で書いた thesis statement を元に、約 1250 語のレポートを書くと仮定し、それぞれの outline を書きな

さい。Reading 1B で紹介した良い論文の４つの特徴や、57 ページで紹介した論文の構成の５つの種類を意識して書きなさい。スペースが不足なら別紙を用いなさい

1.

2.

3.

Applications 3B: Making an Outline

ここまでの Applications では、論文を書くための下準備をしてきた。実際の執筆に入る前に Applications 2B-2（46ページ）で作った brainstorming sheet または mindmap をもとに outline を書きなさい。その時にレポートの構成が論理的かどうか、必要な資料があるかどうか等を確かめながら作成しなさい。スペースが不足なら別紙を用いなさい。

Writing for Fun 3: Resumes / Curriculum Vitae (CVs)

　よく日本人の友人や学生に「英文履歴書[2]を書いたのでチェックして」と頼まれる。履歴書はその国の文化、特に仕事に対する価値観を反映しているので、国によって求められる内容・形式がかなり違う。アメリカで使われている履歴書の形式はさまざまであるが、その中から筆者が使っている形式を紹介したい。まず、下記の英文履歴書を読み、普通の和文履歴書との違いをリストアップしなさい。

アメリカの履歴書	和文履歴書

2　1-2ページの履歴書のことをアメリカではresume といい、イギリスでは主に curriculum vitae (C.V.) というようである。アメリカでいうcurriculum vitae (C.V.)は主に大学教員や研究者が使用する研究業績を含む何ページ（何十ページの場合もよくある）にも渡るものである。ちなみに、日本語でいうレジュメ（配布資料）はアメリカ英語ではhandoutという。

SACHIKO YAMADA

Current Address:
1-1-1-101 Usagi
Tama-ku, Kawasaki-shi,
Kanagawa-ken 210 JAPAN
TEL/FAX (044)111-1111
e-mail: tyamada@aqu.keio.ac.jp

Permanent Address:
1-1-1 Kaizuka
Miyamae-ku, Kawasaki-shi
Kanagawa-ken 216 JAPAN
TEL/FAX (044)111-1111

OBJECTIVE: A challenging teaching position that will utilize my knowledge and experience in teaching English.

EDUCATION:

B.A.   **Keio University Correspondence Course – Faculty of Letters – Tokyo, Japan**
MAJOR: English
G.P.A.:[3]   3.5   Prospective Date of Graduation: March, 1999

RELATED EMPLOYMENT AND EXPERIENCE:

**Sony English School – Tokyo, Japan
(April 1996 to present)**
<u>Head English Instructor</u> – Report directly to the general manager. Responsible for coordinating classes for over 400 students. Supervise over the 5 full-time and 25 part-time teaching staff. Proposed, designed and implemented a 3-day teacher training course resulting in significant improvement in customer satisfaction ratings (from 3.5 to 4.5 on a scale of 1–5).

---

3   G.P.A.は grade point average の略。Aは4、Bは3、Cは2でDは1として平均数値を出したもの。ただし成績が良く（3.5以上）ない限り、いれない方がよい。

English Tutor – Tokyo, Japan
(April 1993 to March 1996)
English Tutor – Tutored four high school students for three years. Helped improve all the students test scores significantly. Three of the students were able to enter their first choice university.

> なるべくsentence は動詞から始めて、活動的な印象を与える

Flower Arrangement Teacher – New York, U.S.A
(April 1990 to March 1993)
Flower Arrangement Teacher – Taught flower arrangements at home to a total of 50 students over a span of 3 years. Learned how to adjust teaching style and methods to the various students who attended. Managed the administrative and financial aspects of operating a small school.

Mukogaoka Elementary School P.T.A. – Kanagawa, Japan
(April 1988 to March 1990)
President of the P.T.A. – Served as president of the P.T.A. at Mukogaoka Elementary School. Responsible for representing over 2,000 parents to the school board. Organized and led monthly P.T.A. meetings.

PERSONAL:
Fluent in Japanese and working knowledge of English. Lived in the United States for 3 years. Qualified flower arrangement teacher.

和文履歴書とアメリカの履歴書の違いは幾つ見つかっただろうか。次表にも幾つか違いをリストアップしたので、参照すること。

アメリカの履歴書	和文履歴書
履歴書用の用紙がない。	履歴書用の用紙がある。
コンピューターで作成したものが望ましい。	手書きが好ましい。
写真はいらない。逆に会社が写真を要求するのは雇用機会均等法に反していることになる。	写真が必要。
誕生日や配偶者・家族の名前等、個人的な情報を書く必要がない。	誕生日や配偶者・家族の名前等、個人的な情報を書く欄がある。
過去の仕事について具体的に書く。	過去の仕事について会社名だけ書けばよい。
自分の性格について書く必要がない。	自分の性格について書く欄がある。

　ここで自分の英文 resume（アメリカ用）を作ってみよう。作成するにあたり、上記の例を参照してもかまわないが英文 resume の書き方の本は多数出ているので1冊入手するとよい。Amazonの検索画面で resume と打ったところ 11907 冊出てきた。インターネット上にも、resume 作成用のホームページも多数あるので、お勧めしたい。インターネット検索で "how to write a resume" または "sample resume" で検索すれば多数のサイトが紹介されている。ビジネス用の履歴書はだいたい1ページに留めるように言われているが、大学の教員や研究者の場合、長くても問題ない。研究者の場合、出版物や研究発表も全て載せるため、何十ページにわたる場合が多い。

Resume を書く際には、次の点を心がけること。

1. Resume は手書きではなく、必ずコンピューターなどで作成したものを使う。
2. 無難さを好む日本の会社と違い、アメリカの会社は個性を求めているの

で、例えば履歴書を白い紙ではなく、ちょっとしゃれた色紙や和紙などに印刷する人も多い。
3. 幾つかの会社を受ける場合は、Objective の欄を応募する position に合わせて変えていく。
4. Objective の部分や今までの仕事内容の解説では、なるべく動詞で sentence を始めることによって活動的なイメージを作りあげることが肝心である。
5. 大学を卒業して何年も経っている場合は Education の欄を履歴書の一番最後に持っていった方がよい。
6. 仕事の経験があまりない場合、アルバイトやボランティアなどから得たスキル等を Related Employment and Experience の欄にいれるとよい。
7. Resume を会社に送る場合、Writing for Fun 4（106ページ～）で紹介する cover letter をつけて送る。

References

Langan, J. (1985). *College writing skills with readings.* New York: McGraw-Hill Book Company.

Oshima, A., & Hogue, A. (1991). *Writing academic English* (2nd ed.). Menlo Park, CA: Addison-Wesley Publishing Company.

CHAPTER 4

Researching: 研究する

Aims:
1. To learn how to conduct a literature review.
2. To learn how to take notes.
3. To learn how to paraphrase, summarize or quote.
4. To learn the APA format of referencing.

4A Conducting a Literature Review
研究者達はどのような研究をしてきたのか

Reading 4A:

Conducting a Literature Review

Once you have a general idea of what you plan to write about, it is time to go to the library to conduct a literature review.[1] A literature review serves two main purposes. First of all, it will reveal to you how much, if any, research has already been done on your topic. You will learn what kinds of studies have already been carried out as well as the results of those studies. Secondly, it will provide you with concrete

---

1 literature review - 文献調査

evidence to support your thesis. Here, let us examine three main ways in which to conduct a literature review: (1) using online library catalogs, (2) using computer databases, and (3) using the reference lists found at the end of articles and books.

The library catalog is useful in locating books that are available within a particular library system. For example, the National Diet Library has its own library catalog called the 国立国会図書館サーチ (http://iss.ndl.go.jp/). This can be used to locate books available at their library as well as other public libraries around Japan. Using their "Advanced search" (詳細検索) option, you can conduct your search based on the Title (タイトル) or Author・Editor (著者・編者). If you do not have a particular book in mind, doing a subject (件名) search is probably best.

Once you have a list of books to look for, you are ready to go to the bookshelves. At the bookshelves, instead of simply taking the books on your list and leaving, take a moment to look around the bookshelves where you found the books. You may be pleasantly surprised to find other books that, for one reason or another,[2] did not show up during your initial search.

The library database is the best way to locate journal articles. Since articles take less time to publish than books, the most recent findings tend to be published as articles before they become books. EBSCO HOST is useful for locating English journal articles while CiNii (http://ci.nii.ac.jp/) is convenient for Japanese ones. Both databases will provide PDF versions of the articles, when available, for immediate download. If a PDF version is not available the library database will often provide options for tracking down the article in your own or nearby library. If the article is not available through your local library system or if you need help locating sources, consult a reference librarian. Today, an increasing number of journal articles can be found online

---

2   for one reason or another - 何らかの理由で

so using a search engine such as Google or Google Scholar can augment what you have already found. When using such general search engines make sure that the article is coming from a reputable journal, magazine, or newspaper, not just someone's webpage, blog or Wikipedia.

After finding relevant books or articles, always look at the "reference list" found at the back of the document to see if there are any other publications that look interesting. Again, you may be pleasantly surprised to find sources that you missed during your initial search.

To access a wide variety of materials, you should not limit your search to English materials. It is not only acceptable but is actually preferable to include materials written in Japanese as well as other languages in which you may be proficient. If you wish to publish your article in an English language journal, your ability to cite studies written in Japanese or other languages will give you an edge over others who can only read English. Journal editors will be more likely to accept your article because it provides references and information that might not have been previously published in English.

Depending on your topic, some of you may find only a few sources. Others may find that it is an unending process. Each article or book leads to several more, which lead to more and so on and so forth. Ideally, a literature review is conducted until there is no more to be found. Realistically, however, the amount of time as well as the limited availability of resources will inevitably limit your search.

What you have found through your literature review should be valuable not only for the research paper you are working on but for future papers as well. For that reason, it is important to keep copies of documents and to file them in an orderly fashion. Make sure to label all the copies with the author's name, title, date, name of journal, name of publisher, as well as other pertinent information so that if you quote it in your paper you can cite it correctly in the reference list.

Conducting a literature review is, perhaps, the most exciting as well as the most time consuming part of working on your research paper. A comprehensive literature review will not only provide you with sufficient background information on your topic but will also give you concrete evidence to use in supporting your thesis statement.

✓ Comprehension Check 4A:

1. What are the two main purposes of a literature review?

2. What are the three main ways in which to conduct a literature review?

3. Is it possible for certain books which are available in the library not to appear through the initial search using the library catalog?

4. If you are looking for books available within the National Diet library system, which search method would you use?

5. If you are looking for journal articles, what search method(s) would you use?

6. What is an advantage to citing journal articles as opposed to books?

7. When writing an English paper, is it acceptable to cite Japanese references? Why or why not?

8. Once you have made copies of pertinent articles or book chapters, what should you do with them?

　Reading 4Aで述べたように、論文のための参考文献等を探すには図書館のコンピューター検索等を使うのが基本となるが、それ以外にも、人という情報源があることを忘れてはいけない。筆者はスランプに陥ると、家族や友人と話してみる。すると意外なところから意外な情報や文献を紹介され、参考になることがある。また、論文を書こうとしている人達と勉強会を作り、経過報告をし合ったり、互いに論文を読み、アドバイスをする場を作ると、精神的にもプラスである。Reading 4A でも述べたように、最近は参考文献がインターネットで簡単に入手できる。筆者も研究室や家から大学の図書館のウェブサイトにアクセスし、学術論文をよくダウンロードしている。また、Google や Google Scholar 経由で学術誌の論文や本の一章を手に入れることもできる。裏ワザとして論文の著者のホームページにアクセスすると論文が無料でダウンロードできることもあり、大変便利になった。

　インターネットのおかげで便利になった反面、入手した資料のなかから信憑性のある文献を、自分でしっかり選ばなくてはならない。Reading 4A では、参考文献として本や学術誌を使い、ウィキペディアや他人のホームページ等を避けるべきと書いたが、ここでは信憑性のある文献とそうでない文献について簡単に説明したい。まずは、「査読あり」と明記されている学術誌の場合、あらかじめその分野の専門家数名が論文を読み、信憑性を評価した上で出版しているので、掲載されている論文は参考文献として相応しい。EBSCO という検索データベースを使う場合は、あらかじめ「査読有り」の論文のみに絞ることもできる。詳しくは図書館の参考係（レファレンスデスク）に相談するとよい。

　書籍の場合、多くの出版社は研究方法論ではなく、売れるかどうかを基準として選んだものを出版する。そのため、本によっては、研究方法論の信憑性が劣る場合もある。また、研究に基づく本の場合、学術誌に発表された論文を、後になってまとめている場合が多いので、学術論文より古い情報が載っている

可能性がある。こうした書籍を参考文献とすること自体には問題はないが、学術論文と比べると質が劣る。ウィキペディアや個人が書いているブログの場合、信頼性をチェックする機能がないため、参考文献としては相応しくない。

4B Taking Notes
メモをとるには

Reading 4B:

Taking Notes

The amount as well as quality of outside resources one cites reflects upon one's skill as a researcher. Locating many relevant outside sources, therefore, is one of the keys to writing a good paper. When citing those sources, however, one must be especially careful to represent the authors accurately. If authors are not given proper credit one is not only violating basic academic ethics but might risk being sued for plagiarism.[3] Unfortunately, plagiarism is not necessarily the result of intentionally copying someone's work. It can occur unintentionally by writing down someone else's idea as if it were one's own. This is more likely to occur if one does not take notes carefully. To avoid this, accurate note-taking is essential. Here, we will discuss three main ways in which information from outside sources are noted and cited: quoting, paraphrasing, and summarizing. When taking notes, it is important to distinguish clearly a quote from a paraphrase or a summary.

Quoting means that a certain author's writing is used word for word. When writing a paper, quotes should be placed between two quotation marks (" ") and followed by the author's last name, year of

---

3   plagiarism - 盗作

publication, and page number(s)[4] (e.g., Van Leunen, 1992, p. 46). In your notes, too, quotation marks should be used to indicate that you have quoted directly.

Short quotes can be used without obtaining permission from the author as long as the quote is cited as indicated above. For longer quotes, the guidelines are vague. According to Turabian (1996), the exact criteria used to determine whether or not it is necessary to obtain permission from the publishers, libraries and others who hold the rights to publications depends on the organization or person who has the rights to the literary works. To be on the safe side, when quoting several paragraphs, entire poems, essays, an illustration, a table or anything of significant length, obtain permission from the author or publisher. Or better still do not do it—other scholars want to read your work—not somebody else's.

According to Van Leunen (1992), because many young scholars worry too much about giving credit to the original author they tend to quote too much. Although credit needs to be given to the originator of an idea or study, this can be done through paraphrasing and summarizing. A quote should only be used when the particular wording in the original adds special significance to your writing. Otherwise, too many quotes can make your writing seem fragmented.[5]

For the most part, when citing outside sources, paraphrasing or summarizing is used. Paraphrasing refers to restating something in your own words. Summarizing is used when condensing[6] a large amount of material. When paraphrasing or summarizing, one must be extremely careful not to change the content of the original. According to APA[7] guidelines, as long as the author's last name and year of publication (e.g.,

---

4 ただし、40 word 以上の quote の場合は一旦改行し、quote 全体を他の行より下げて挿入する。10行以上の場合はなるべく quote せず paraphrase か summarize するように (Amato, 1995)。
5 fragmented - バラバラで統一性がない
6 condense - 要約する
7 American Psychological Association の略。〈詳しくは 4C を参照〉

CHAP
4

Researching

Van Leunen, 1992) are cited in the manuscript and the full reference is cited in the reference list, permission need not be obtained when paraphrasing or summarizing.

There are two frequently used methods with which researchers organize their notes. One way is to use a highlighter, a pen, and post-its and take notes directly on the article. Recently, software such as iAnnotate PDF or ez Annotate enable you to take notes and highlight directly on an iPad or computer. Whether you use a hard copy or an e-copy, the advantage to this method is speed and accuracy as it eliminates the need to quote or paraphrase. The other way is to input your notes directly onto a computer (see Figure 4.1). When taking notes, some researchers prefer to jot down the paraphrased or summarized version while others prefer to copy the original as a quote and save the paraphrasing or summarizing for later. The advantage of the former method is that it saves time and space. The advantage of the latter is accuracy. If you choose the latter method, remember to use quotation marks so that you will be able to differentiate direct quotes from something that has already been paraphrased or summarized. The advantage of taking notes on a computer is that you can easily copy[8] segments and paste[9] it onto your article, rearrange your notes, or use the search[10] command to find specific information.

Note-taking, although a little tedious at first, is an essential part of the literature review. Well-organized notes not only make it possible to cite accurately from a large number of sources but will be useful when writing future reports or articles on a similar subject.

---

8 コンピューター用語で「コピー」するというのは入力したデータの全体または一部を複写することである。
9 「ペースト」する、というのは「コピー」した部分を好きな場所に挿入することである。
10 「サーチ」（検索）機能というのはキーワードを打ち込むことによってその言葉を検索する機能のことである。

✓ Comprehension Check 4B:

1. What do you need to be careful of when citing outside sources?

2. Is it possible for an honest student to inadvertently plagiarize?

3. "A fallacy of some repute and some duration is the one which assumes that because a student can write an adequate essay in his native language, he can necessarily write an adequate essay in a second language" (**Kaplan, 1966**).
What is missing in the citation（太字になっている部分）of the above quote?

4. Why is it important not to quote excessively?

5. If you are planning to use a short quote from a book do you need to obtain permission from the publisher?

6. Besides quoting, what are the two other methods in which information from outside sources are used?

7. When paraphrasing or summarizing, is it necessary to obtain permission from the author?

8. When taking notes, what is the main advantage of paraphrasing or summarizing it? What is the main disadvantage?

9. What are the two frequently used methods to organize notes?

_____

_____

> ⭐ **Figure 4.1: Taking Notes on a Computer**

Turabian, K. L. (Revised by Grossman, J. & Bennett, A.) (1996). *A manual for writers of term papers, theses and dissertations* (6th ed.). Chicago, ILL: The University of Chicago Press.   ← Reference list に必要な情報をまず書く。

　*　"Quotations involving more than a few contiguous paragraphs or stanzas, and the use of anything in its entirety—a poem, an essay, a letter, a section of a book, an illustration, or sometimes a table—may exceed the limits of "fair use" as defined by the Copyright Act of 1976. Publishers, libraries, and others who hold the rights to literary works do not interpret fair use uniformly." (pp. 73-74)   ← 使えそうな部分。引用の場合はこのように引用符の中にいれ、ページ番号を記す。

　*　According to the Copyright Act of 1976, long quotations such as multiple consecutive paragraphs, an entire essay, a letter, a book section, an illustration or a table may be considered plagiarism although the exact details vary depending on who has the rights.   ← 自分の言葉に言い換えている場合は引用符もページ番号も必要ない。

84

Quoting

参考文献から直接引用する場合、一番単純なパターンとして引用符（" "）で囲み、その後に（ ）内に著者名、出版年、ページ数を書く方法がある。それ以外にも色々な引用の仕方があるのでここで紹介しよう。

1. 長い文を全て引用せずに部分的に使ってつなげる場合は省略した部分を明示するために...を使う。例えば：

   "I went for years not finishing anything. Because of course, when you finish something you can be judged . . . I had poems which were re-written so many times. I suspect it was just a way of avoiding sending them out" (Erica Jong, as cited in Charlton, 1997, p. 101).

2. 引用文の省略などによって文法的にズレが生じた場合、[ ]内に言葉を入れて読みやすくする。例えば：

   . . . [he] said that . . . [it] is actually . . .

3. 前述の通り、引用は原文の言葉を使うことに強い意義がない限り、避けるのが無難である。さらに、引用する部分を最小限に減らすために部分的に paraphrase（言い換え）し、部分的に引用することも多い。例えば原文 (a) の前半を paraphrase し、後半だけ引用したものとして (b)：

   (a) "The concept that no two people see exactly the same thing when actively using their eyes in a natural situation is shocking to some people because it implies that not all men relate to the world around them in the same way" (Hall, 1982, p. 69).

   ↓

   (b) According to Hall (1982), the fact that different people perceive the external world differently "is shocking to some people because it implies that not all men relate to the world around them in the same way" (p. 69).

Useful Expressions 4B:

Paraphrasing や summarizing をする時には、文章自体には研究者の名前等はいれず、文末に（　）で囲み、研究者名と出版年のみを入れることが多い。例えば：

> Classroom behavior is not the same worldwide. Behavior and expectations held by students and teachers are strongly influenced by culture (Hofstede, Hofstede and Minkov, 2010).

1人の研究者からの情報を複数の文章で伝える場合は、各文章の後に研究者名を入れずに、一通り書き終えたところにつける（上記を参照）。もし、その情報が幾つものパラグラフにわたる場合は、各パラグラフの最後に研究者名と出版年を入れる。

それ以外にも文章中に研究者名等を入れることもある。その時によく使う表現等を幾つかここで紹介する。

他の研究者の意見等に言及する	
According to Jones (20xx) . . .	Jones (20xx) によると…
Jones (20xx) *claims* that . . .	Jones (20xx) は＿＿だと主張している。
Jones (20xx) *states* that . . .	Jones (20xx) は＿＿だと述べている。
Jones (20xx) *indicates* that . . .	Jones (20xx) は＿＿だと指摘している。
Jones (20xx) *introduces* . . .	Jones (20xx) は＿＿を紹介している。

Some researchers *argue* that . . . (i.e.,*Jones, 20xx; Smith, 20xx).	研究者によっては＿＿だと論じる人もいる(i.e., Jones, 20xx; Smith, 20xx)。
Jones (20xx) *argues* that . . .	Jones (20xx) は＿＿だと論じている／主張している。
Jones (20xx) *contends* that . . .	Jones (20xx) は＿＿だと強く主張している。
Jones (20xx) *emphasizes* that . . .	Jones (20xx) は＿＿だと強調している。
Many authors (e.g.,** Jones, 20xx; Kennedy, 20xx; Smith, 20xx) have *emphasized* that . . .	多くの研究者(e.g., Jones, 20xx; Kennedy, 20xx; Smith, 20xx) は＿＿だと強く主張してきた。
Jones (20xx) *suggests* that . . .	Jones (20xx) は＿＿だと提案している。
Jones (20xx) (first) *proposed* . . .	(初めて)＿＿を提案したのは Jones (20xx) である。
Although Jones (20xx) . . ., he *recognizes* that . . .	Jones (20xx) は＿＿だが、＿＿ということは認めている。
Jones (20xx) *contests* Smith's (20xx) argument . . .	Jones (20xx) は Smith (20xx) の議論について＿＿と異議を唱えている。
As Jones (20xx) *makes clear* . . .	Jones (20xx) が＿＿を明らかにしたように...
Jones (20xx) *advocates* that . . .	Jones (20xx) は＿＿を支持している。
Jones (20xx) *notes* that . . .	Jones (20xx) は＿＿に言及している。
Jones (20xx) *points out* that . . .	Jones (20xx) は＿＿だと指摘している。

研究結果を報告する

Jones (20xx) (has) *found* that . . .	Jones (20xx) は＿だとわかった。
Research has *revealed* that . . . (Jones, 20xx).	＿だと研究によって明らかにされた (Jones, 20xx)。
An example of ＿ is *provided* by Jones' (20xx) study of ＿.	＿についての一例は、Jones (20xx) の＿の研究によって与えられている。
Jones (20xx) *demonstrated* a link between ＿ and ＿.	Jones (20xx) は＿と＿の関係を論証した。
A survey conducted by Jones (20xx) *resulted* in . . .	Jones (20xx) の調査は＿という結果になった。
In a study of ＿, research *indicated* that . . . (Jones, 20xx).	＿の研究の結果、＿だということがわかった (Jones, 20xx)。
Jones (20xx) *investigated* the relationship between ＿ and ＿.	Jones (20xx) は＿と＿の関係について調査した。
Jones (20xx) *attempted* to identify . . .	Jones (20xx) は＿を見極めることを試みた。
Jones (20xx) *attempted* to establish . . .	Jones (20xx) は＿を立証しようと企てた。
Jones (20xx) *explored* . . .	Jones (20xx) は＿を探究した。
Jones (20xx) *examined* . . .	Jones (20xx) は＿を調査した。
Jones (20xx) *conducted* interviews with . . .	Jones (20xx) は＿を対象にインタビュー調査をした。
Jones (20xx) also *found* evidence supporting . . .	Jones (20xx) も＿を裏付ける証拠を見つけた。
Jones (20xx) *found* that . . .	Jones (20xx) は＿を見出した。

例を挙げる	
Jones (20xx), for example, *reports* that . . .	例えば、Jones (20xx) は＿＿だと報告している。
For example, Jones (20xx) *proposes* that . . .	例えば、Jones (20xx) は＿＿だと提案している。
その他	
Jones (20xx) *distinguishes* between＿and＿.	Jones (20xx) は＿と＿をはっきり区別している。
Jones (20xx) *elaborates* on the . . .	Jones (20xx) が＿について詳しく述べている。
Jones (20xx) *extended* Smith's (20xx) theory of . . .	Jones (20xx) はSmith (20xx) の＿＿学説を広げた。
Jones (20xx) *developed* a model of . . .	Jones (20xx) が＿についてのモデルを提案した。
Jones (20xx) *defines*＿as＿.	Jones (20xx) は＿を＿と定義している。

＊ "i.e.," は「すなわち」という意味である。ラテン語の *id est* の略である。この様に複数ある場合、アルファベットの順に並べる

＊＊ "e.g.," は「例えば」という意味である。ラテン語の *exempli grati*a の略である

Exercise 4B-1: Paraphrasing & Summarizing

　86 〜 89 ページの表現の一覧の中には、Reading 1B（14 〜 19 ページ）で使われているものも幾つかある。Reading 1B をもう一度読み直し、86 〜 89 ページにある表現には丸をしなさい。

Exercise 4B-2: Paraphrasing & Summarizing

　92 〜 95 ページの 5 つの文章を読み、自分の言葉で言い換え（paraphrase）なさい。言い換える際にどの様な手順をとるかは人それぞれであるが、1 つの方法として次のやり方がある。

　ステップ 1　原文を何度も読み、理解する。
　ステップ 2　原文を見ないで、自分の言葉で言い換える。
　ステップ 3　原文と言い換えた文を比べ、内容が正確に伝わっているかを確認し、必要に応じて調整する。

　言い換える時には原文のキーワードを幾つかそのまま使ってもかまわない。類語辞典[11]を活用すると便利である。ただし、類語辞典に出ていても、知らない言葉を使うと不自然な文章になる場合があるので、注意すること。

　また、次の例にならい、要約（summary）も作ってみよう。

11　類語辞典を英語で thesaurus という。代表的なものとしては Roget 社のものがあるが、筆者は Random House College Edition を使っている。

Example:

Original: "Women who have children in their 40s have a greater chance of living to be 100 than those who give birth earlier. The ability of late mothers[12] to reproduce may indicate a slower aging process in such women and serve as a marker of longevity"[13] ("Health report," 1997, September 22, p. 18).

Paraphrase (良い例): **Research has revealed that** there is a greater chance for women who give birth in their 40s to live until they are 100 compared to those who give birth at a younger age. The fact that they are able to give birth late in their life might be an indication that their aging process is slower. In other words, being able to give birth at an older age might be a sign of longevity ("Health report," 1997, September 22, p. 18).

このようにキーワード以外はすべて言い換えているものは○とする。

Paraphrase (悪い例): Those who have a greater chance of living to be 100 are women who have children in their 40s compared to those who give birth earlier. An indication of a slower aging process in such women and a marker of longevity is the ability of late mothers to reproduce ("Health report," 1997, September 22, p. 18).

このように文章の前後を入れ替えただけでは盗作となる。

Summary: **Research has indicated that** ability to give birth at a later age might be an indicator of longevity ("Health report," 1997, September 22, p. 18).

要約は原文より短く。

---

12 late mother - 高齢出産者
13 longevity - 長生き

1.

Original: "Exercise is almost invariably better for your back than anything else you can put onto or into your body. Compared with all other back-pain treatments, exercise makes the most sense because it is harmless, affordable, and effective.

The same cannot be said of painkillers[14] and anti-inflammatory medications,[15] for example, although these drugs are routinely prescribed for people with back pain. Indeed, drugs constitute the most widely used treatment for back pain. As we discovered in our Back Pain Survey and related research for our book, Backache Relief, they do practically no good at all, and their unpleasant side effects[16] may cause considerable harm" (Sobel & Klein, 1996, p. 11).

Paraphrase:

Summary:

---

14 painkiller - 鎮痛剤
15 anti-inflammatory medication - 炎症を抑える薬
16 side effect - 副作用

2.

Original: "An early report from France—where else?—finds more reason to enjoy wine. For reasons that are still unclear, drinking it daily—in moderation—may help stave off[17] Alzheimer's disease"[18] ("Health report," 1997, April, p.14).

Paraphrase:

Summary:

3.

Original: "People who socialize a lot seem to get fewer colds, even though they're probably exposed to more germs. Why? Researchers suspect a support network[19] may help keep immune systems[20] strong" ("Health report," 1997, July, p.14).

Paraphrase:

---

17 stave off - くい止める
18 Alzheimer's disease - アルツハイマー病
19 support network - 心の交流
20 immune system - 免疫

Summary:

4. Original: "Pregnant women, steer clear of [21] smoke. Exposure to **PASSIVE SMOKE**—even small amounts—can significantly increase the odds[22] of giving birth to a baby whose lungs don't function properly. The damage begins in utero[23] when chemicals from cigarette smoke cause less oxygen to go from mother to fetus"[24] ("Health report," 1997, April, p. 16).

Paraphrase:

Summary:

---
21 steer clear of - 避ける
22 odds - 確率
23 in utero - 子宮の中で
24 fetus - 胎児

5.

Original: "More important than the chair you sit in is the amount of time you spend sitting. Since sitting offers more opportunity for back aggravation than either standing or lying down, you may need to limit your sitting time. Whenever possible, break up long sits by getting up to stretch. You can do this most easily at home, of course, but try to stretch at work, too. If you're driving on a long car trip, let yourself stop frequently for stretch breaks. On long plane flights, too, look for times when you can move about in the aisles, and seize the opportunity"[25] (Sobel & Klein, 1996, pp. 179-180).

Paraphrase:

Summary:

---

25 seize the opportunity - 機会を逃がさずにつかむ

「出典を明らかにするように」と学生にいくら指示しても、多くの場合、文章を直接引用したもの (quote) のみに限り、出典を明示してくる。学術論文の場合、「具体的な情報」は必ず出典を明らかにすることになっている。「具体的な情報」とは統計データ、人の考え、理論、研究結果等を含む。「そんなの当たり前」だと思う情報でも、情報源を明らかにしなくてはならない。例えば、「日本人はよく集団主義だと言われている」という文章を書く場合でも必ず出典を書かなければならない。何故ならば、研究によって違う結果が出ている場合も多々あるからだ。実際、多くの研究によると日本人は集団主義だという結果を出しているが (e.g., Condon, 1984; DeMente, 1995; Hofstede, Hofstede, & Minkov, 2010) 反対の結果を出している論文も少なくない (See Takano & Osaka, 1999 for a review)。そのためにも、一見当たり前だと思う情報でも必ず出典を明らかにする必要がある。

ここでReading 1Bを読み返しながら、どの文章には出典が明示されていて、どの文章には明示されていないかを分析して欲しい。ここでは初めのparagraphのみについて解説するが、自分でも続けて分析するように。

まずは、冒頭はquoteなので出典先とページ数が明示してある。そして、次の文章でKaplan (1966) の考えが述べてあるので、その旨明示している。続く文章でKaplan (1966) の考えを著者が言い換えているのが明らかに分かるので、明示する必要はない。次の文章では "some researchers" と書いてあるので複数明示しなくてはならない。ちなみに、複数の研究がなされているうちの幾つかだけ示す場合は "e.g.," (例えば) と書いてから幾つか羅列する。もし、複数の研究が限られた数しかない場合は "i.e.," (すなわち) と書き、全て明示する。

次の文章では "some studies" と書いてあるがその次の文章で具体的な出典 (i.e., Taylor & Chen, 1991) があるので、出典は必要ない。残りの文章では基本的にそこまでに書いたことを言い換えたり、まとめたりしているので出典は必要ない。一番最後の文章ではLangan (1985) の提示している「良い論文の特徴」について語っているのでその旨明示している。

4C Referencing
使った文献を明示するには

　分野、学術誌により参考文献表の書き方は異なるが、アメリカでは心理学、社会学、ビジネス等では APA（American Psychological Association）スタイルが主に使われている。文学などでは MLA（Modern Language Association）が主であるので、文学専攻の場合は MLA Handbook for Writers of Research Papers を参照するとよい。また、分野によっては Chicago Style が主となっている。シカゴ・スタイルについてはトゥラビアン著、沼口と沼口[訳]の『シカゴ・スタイル研究論文執筆マニュアル』（慶應義塾大学出版会）を参照するといい。多数の論文を書く場合は EndNote[26] 等の bibliographic database ソフトを使うことにより、必要な情報をコンピューター画面の指示通りに入力すると、それを自動的に APA や MLA 等の基準に合わせてフォーマッティングできるので便利である。このようなソフトを使うことにより、1つの論文を幾つか違う分野の出版社に出す場合、簡単に APA から MLA に変えることができるのは画期的である。さらに、コンピューターに書誌情報を入力することで、自分のための参考文献データベースを作ることができ、他の論文を書く時にも再利用できるという利点がある。この様な有料ソフト以外にもインターネット上の無料ソフトもある。例えば Son of Citation Machine [http://citationmachine.net/] を使い、APA 方式を選ぶだけで簡単に参考文献を APA スタイルにフォーマットできる。

　APA スタイルでは参考文献を脚注で表示せずに本文中に著者の姓、出版年等を（　）で囲み挿入することになっている。Reading 1B は APA スタイルで書かれているのでそれを参照するとよい。文末の文献リストの作り方の詳細については Publication Manual of the American Psychological Association 6th Edition を参照するとよいが、ここでも簡単に紹介しよう。
　インターネット経由で入手した文献の電子版の多くには Digital Object

---

26 EndNote 以外に Biblio-Links、Pro-cite、Reference Manager 等と色々な bibliographic database がある。筆者は EndNote Plus を長年愛用している。EndNote は日本では USACO Corporation（http://www.usaco.co.jp）から購入できる。

Identifiers (DOI) 番号というものがついているので、Reference に明示する。DOI がある場合は論文の一番上の部分に表記されている（下記を参照）。電子版でも DOI 番号がない場合は URL を明示する。

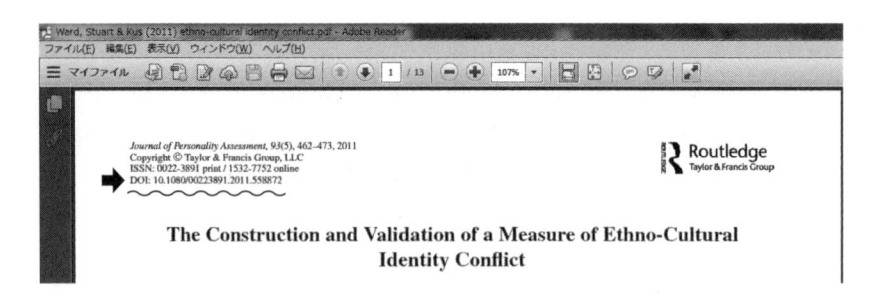

インターネットから入手した文献の出典の表記については、Publication Manual of the American Psychological Association 6th Edition に加えて、APA Style Guide to Electronic References, 6th edition (2012) が参考になる。また、以下のサイトにも簡単な説明がある：https://owl.english.purdue.edu/owl/resource/560/10/

本の場合：

● 姓, 名のイニシャル．（ミドルネームのイニシャル．）(発行年). 本の題名（イタリック字体）. 発行所：出版社名.

外国の方の名前の場合、どちらが姓でどちらが名が分からない場合がある。大体、Tomoko Yoshida と羅列して書かれている場合は最初が名、後が姓である。Yoshida, Tomoko とカンマが間にある場合は最初が姓、あとが名。また、Tomoko YOSHIDA 等とどちらかが全て大文字の場合は大文字で書かれているものが姓である。

Reference で題名を書く際に特に指定がない場合は冒頭の文字のみを大文字で書き、残り（固有名詞以外）は小文字で書くように。

1. Oshima, A., & Hogue, A. (2006). *Writing academic English* (4th ed.*). White Plains, NY: Pearson Education, Inc.

*：第 2 版以降は 2nd ed. 3rd ed. 4th ed. 等とつける。その部分はイタリック字体にしない。

文章中の表記の例：Oshima and Hogue (2006) suggest that...又は "Every good paragraph has..." (Oshima & Hogue, 2006, p. 4).

本の中の 1 章の場合：
- 姓，名のイニシャル．（ミドルネームのイニシャル．)（発行年)．章の題名．In 編者の名のイニシャル．（ミドルネームのイニシャル．）姓(Ed. または複数の場合は Eds.[27])，本の題名（イタリック字体）（pp.*ページ）．発行所：出版社名．

> 紙媒体の場合はこの様に出版場所：出版社と明記する。電子版の場合は下記のいずれの方法で明記する。
> 1) doi:xx.xxxx/xxxxxxxxxx
> 2) Retrieved from http://www.xxxxxxxx

2. Bhawuk, D. P. S. (2012). Diversity and intercultural communication: The influence of individualism and collectivism. In E. Christopher (Ed.), *Communication across cultures* (pp.42-53). UK: Palgrave Macmillan.

文章中の表記の例：Bhawuk (2012) proposes … 又は … (Bhawuk, 2012).

3a. Okabe, R. (1993). Nihon no rhetoric [Japan's rhetoric]. In M. Hashimoto & S. Ishii (Eds.), *Nihonjin no communication [Japanese communication styles*] (pp. 55-81). Tokyo: Kirihara-shoten.

3b. Okabe, R. (1993). 日本のレトリック [Japan's rhetoric]**. In M. Hashimoto & S. Ishii (Eds.), 日本人のコミュニケーション [*Japanese communication styles*] (pp. 55-81). Tokyo: Kirihara-shoten.

*：ページが複数ある場合はページを表わす数字の前に pp. と書く。単数の場合は p. とする。
**：海外の学術誌などに論文を送る場合は、日本語の文献名をローマ字で記し、その後の [ ] の中に英語訳をいれる（3aを参照）。ただし日本で出版する場合はAPAスタイルでは決まっていないが文献名は日本語で記し、その後の [ ] の中に英語訳をいれた方がより親切である（3bを参照）。ただし、これも学術誌によるのであらかじめ確認すること。

文章中の表記の例：Okabe (1993) states that … 又は … (Okabe, 1993).

---

27 Ed. = Editor; Eds. = Editors

学術誌の中の論文の場合：
- 姓, 名のイニシャル.（ミドルネームのイニシャル.）(発行年). 論文の題名. 学術誌の題名（title case*で）, 発行番号（イタリック字体）, ページ.

4. Ward, C., Stuart, J., & Kus, L. (2011). The construction and validation of a measure of ethno-cultural identity conflict. *Journal of Personality Assessment, 93(5),* 462-473. doi: 10.1080/00223891.2011.558872

＊：Title case とは単語の先頭文字はすべて大文字、ただし冠詞・前置詞等は小文字というスタイル（詳しくは166〜167ページを参照）。
＊＊：発行番号がわかる場合はページを表わす数字の前に pp. と書く必要はない。

文章中の表記の例：Ward, Stuart, and Kus (2011) argue... 又は... (Ward, Stuart, & Kus, 2011).

> 複数の著者の場合、初めての引用の場合のみ全員の姓を明記する。二回目以降は Ward et al. (2011) と筆頭著者名のみを明記する。ただし、著者が6名以上の場合は初めての引用のでも Ward et al. (2011) と筆頭著者名のみを明記する。

雑誌の中の記事の場合：
- 姓, 名のイニシャル.（ミドルネームのイニシャル.）(発行年月). 記事の題名.雑誌の題名（title caseで）, 発行番号（わかる場合は入れる）（イタリック字体）, ページ.

5. Barker, E. (2014, April). 7 things the most interesting people all have in common. Time. Retrieved from http://time.com/

> インターネットで入手した場合、URL を明記する。記事の URL は変動するため、雑誌のホームページの URL を明記するとよい。

文章中の表記の例：Barker (2014) states that... 又は... (Barker, 2014).

新聞記事：
- 姓, 名のイニシャル.（ミドルネームのイニシャル.）(発行年月日). 記事の題名. 新聞名（title case でイタリック字体）, p. ページ.（インターネット版の場合はページ番号は省き、Retrieved from と書き、URL を記す。）

6a. 紙媒体：Clavel, T. (2014, May 11). Returnees' experiences drive a will to give something back. *The Japan Times,* p. 10.

6b. インターネット版：Clavel, T. (2014, May 11). Returnees' experiences drive a will to give something back. *The Japan Times*. Retrieved from http://www.japantimes.co.jp/

文章中の表記の例： Clavel (2014) gave many examples of ... 又は、 ... (Clavel, 2014).

Exercise 4C-1: Referencing

上記1～6で扱った参考文献について下記の質問に答えなさい。

1. Reference #1 What is the last name of the second author?

2. Reference #1 When was this book published?

3. Reference #2 What is the name of the publisher?

4. Reference #2 Where was the book published?

5. Reference #3 What does "Eds." mean?

6. Reference #3 Is this a book, a book chapter or a journal article?

7. Reference #4 What is the name of the article?

8. Reference #4 Which journal was this article published in?

9. Reference #5 What is the name of the article?

10. Reference #6 Which newspaper was this published in?

Exercise 4C-2: Referencing

下記の文献を APA スタイルに沿って記入せよ。特に題名等の大文字／小文字に注意するように。日本語で書かれている文献の場合、ローマ字（海外で出版する場合）もしくは日本語（日本の学術誌に出版する場合）で表記し [ ] の中に英語で表記する。

1. 本の題名：異文化トレーニング：ボーダレス社会を生きる [Intercultural training: Living in a borderless society]　著者：Kyoko Yashiro, Eriko Machi, Hiroko Koike, Tomoko Yoshida, [八代京子, 町惠理子, 小池浩子, 吉田友子]　発行年：2009　出版場所：Tokyo　出版社：Sanshusha

2. 本の題名：With Respect to the Japanese: A Guide for Americans　著者：John C. Condon, Tomoko Masumoto　発行年：2011　出版場所：Boston, MA　出版社：Intercultural Press

3. 論文記事の題名：The debate about cultural difference: deep culture, cultural identity, and culture's influence on behavior.　論文の著者：Shaules, Joseph　学術誌名：Journal of Intercultural Communication [異文化コミュニケーション]　発行年月：2007　発行番号：10　ページ：115-132

4. 雑誌記事の題名：部下が悪いのか？―多様化する職場の中でのコミュニケーション [Is it the subordinate's fault?: Communication in an increasingly multicultural work environment]
記事の著者：鈴木有香 [Suzuki, Yuka]　　雑誌名：人事院月報 [National Personnel Authority Monthly Reports]　　発行年月日：2010, June
ページ：36-39

5. 本の題名：The Japanese Overseas: Can they go home again?
著者：White, Merry　　発行年：1988　　出版場所：London
出版社：The Free Press

6. 論文名：異文化適応のメカニズム―文化人類学的考察　[The Mechanism of Cultural Adaptation: An Anthropological Study]　論文の著者：Ebuchi, K. [江淵一公]　学術誌名：教育と医学　[Education and Medicine]　発行年：1986　発行番号：10　ページ：910-948

7. 本の章の題名：Psychological perspectives: social psychology, language, and intercultural communication 章の著者：Madeleine Brabant, Bernadette Watson, & Cindy Gallois, ページ：55-76　本の題名：Handbook of Intercultural Communication　編者：Helga Kotthoff, & Spencer-Helen Oatey, 発行年：2007　出版場所：Berlin, Germany
出版社：Mouton de Gruyter

8. 論文名：Conflicting acculturation strategies regarding ethnocultural diversity: Towards a resolution for Japan's multicultural future. 論文の著者：Komisarof, Adam　学術誌名：Journal of Intercultural Communication [異文化コミュニケーション]　発行年：2010　発行番号：13　ページ：31-38

9. 本の題名：異文化ミスコミュニケーション [Intercultural Miscommunication]　著者：Muro, Mary.　発行年：2001　出版場所：Tokyo　出版社：Seibido

Exercise 4C-3:　Using a Library Search Engine

　この Exercise は国立国会図書館サーチ（http://iss.ndl.go.jp/）を使って文献を調べる練習である。Exercise 4C-2 の 2〜9 の文献全てを国立国会図書館サーチで調べ、1 の例を参考に詳細を下欄に記入してみよう。(注意：詳細検索を使い、検索内容を打ち込む時にはなるべく特徴のあるキーワードを打ち込むとよい。あまりにも漠然としたキーワードを入力してしまうと、該当する文献がありすぎて、膨大な数の検索結果が出てしまう。例えば 10 番の場合、"Japan" と打ってしまうと 969566 の文献が表示される。この場合には、"Japan as number one" または "Vogel, Ezra" などで検索したほうがよい。著者名が分かる場合は、まずそこから検索をスタートするとよい。また、論文や雑誌記事を検索している場合は、論文名や雑誌記事の題名ではなく、学術誌名や雑誌名で検索すること。本の一章を探す場合も、章の題名ではなく本の題

名で検索すること。)

例：
1. 所蔵場所　　　東京本館書庫　　　請求記号　EC235-J185

2. 所蔵場所　　　_____　　　請求記号　_____
3. 所蔵場所　　　_____　　　請求記号　_____
2. 所蔵場所　　　_____　　　請求記号　_____
4. 所蔵場所　　　_____　　　請求記号　_____
5. 所蔵場所　　　_____　　　請求記号　_____
6. 所蔵場所　　　_____　　　請求記号　_____
7. 所蔵場所　　　_____　　　請求記号　_____
8. 所蔵場所　　　_____　　　請求記号　_____

Applications 4C:　　Researching

　ここで Applications 3B（69 ～ 70 ページ）で作成した outline を見ながら、Applications 2C（51 ページ）で作成した論文の thesis statement（命題）をサポートするのに必要な資料や文献を考えてみる。その他に、先行研究も含めて図書館等で資料調査を開始しよう。調べ方は Reading 4A を参考にし、見つけた文献はすべて論文自体に書き込むかコンピューターに直接入力しておく。ノートを取る段階で quote なのか paraphrase または summary なのかがはっきりわかるように明示しておく。文献名等は 97 ページ以下で紹介した APA スタイルを用いること。

　資料調べの結果、思ったような資料が見つからなかったり、逆に意外な資料が見つかったりして、論文の方向性が根本的に変わることもあり得る。従ってこの時点で、もう一度、論文の内容や構成について考え直し、必要であれば outline を作り直すこと。

Writing for Fun 4:　Cover Letters

　履歴書を作成し、会社に送付する際に、履歴書の中で特に強調したい自分の長所や仕事経験などを、送り状のなかで改めてアピールすることができる。こうした送り状を英語では cover letter[28]という。形式は通常の business letter と同じだが、履歴書につける cover letter を書く際には、自分の経歴や経験に具体的に言及しつつ、自分が応募（apply）している職業にいかにふさわしく、適任であるかを強調し、相手に自分を印象づけることが大事である。手紙はあくまでもポジティブな面を強調して書くように。マイナスなことでも視点を変えればプラスになることもあるので、工夫して書くこと。インターネット検索で"cover letter resume"と入力すればたくさんの例が出てくるので、参照するように。

　Cover letter に必要な要素として下記の4つがある。
1. なぜその会社に応募したいかを説明する。
2. 自分の転職または就職の動機を説明する。
3. 簡単に自分の経歴を説明し、特になぜ自分が適任者かを誰もが納得できるように主張する。
4. 返事の依頼、その手間に対する感謝の言葉、直接会って話をしたいことをアピールするのも大切である。

---

[28] 履歴書以外にも、論文を学術誌に送る時や仕事上のパンフレットを送る場合等にも、cover letter が必要である。

1-1-1 Usagi,
Tama-ku, Kawasaki-shi
Kanagawa-ken Japan 210-0003
January 4, 2015

Ms. Mary Johnson
Director of Human Resources
Sam's Language School
1-1-1 Tatsumi, Chiyoda-ku
Tokyo 111

Dear Ms. Johnson:

    I have been interested in Sam's Language School ever since I read an article about its unique curriculum over a year ago. I was, therefore, extremely excited to see your advertisement placed in today's The Japan Times.

    As can be seen in my resume, I am presently the Head English Instructor for Sony English School. Although I have enjoyed my job immensely, I feel ready for a position with further responsibility. Hence, my interest in applying for the position as the "Director of the English Teaching Section."

    Upon reading the job description for the position, I feel I have the skills and experiences required. I not only have extensive experience teaching English, but have also designed and implemented teacher training courses for our staff. As I understand, Sam's Language School caters to a wide range of clients, including junior high school students, business people, and housewives. Through my experience as a tutor, flower arrangement teacher, mother and president of the P.T.A., I am confident that I can help cater to the various needs of your clients.

    Although my resume is as comprehensive as possible, it cannot fully convey my qualifications and experience. I would, therefore, appreciate the opportunity to meet with you in person and talk to you about the position.

    Thank you for your consideration. I look forward to hearing from you soon.

Sincerely yours,

Sachiko Yamada

Sachiko Yamada

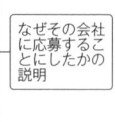

References

Amato, C. J. (1995). *The world's easiest guide to using the APA.* Westminster, CA: Stargazer.

American Psychological Association. (2009). *Publication manual of the American Psychological Association* (6th ed.). Washington DC: Author.

Charlton, J. (Ed.). (1997). *The writer's quotation book: A literary companion.* Winchester, MA: Faber & Faber.

Condon, J.C. (1984). *With respect to the Japanese.* Yarmouth, ME: Intercultural Press Inc.

De Mente, B.L. (1995). *Japanese etiquette & ethics in business* (6th ed.). Lincolnwood, ILL: NTC Books.

Hall, E. T. (1982). *The hidden dimension.* New York, NY: Anchor Books Doubleday.

Health report. (1997, April 7). Time. p.14.

Health report. (1997, April 14). Time. p.16.

Health report. (1997, July 7). Time. p.14.

Health report (1997, September 15). Time. p.14.

Health report (1997, September 22). Time. p.18.

Hofstede, G.H., Hofstede, G.J., & Minkov, M. (2010). *Cultures and Organizations: Software of the Mind: Intercultural Cooperation and Its Importance for Survival.* New York, NY: McGraw-Hill.

Kaplan, R. B. (1966). Cultural thought patterns in intercultural education. *Language Learning: A Journal of Applied Linguistics,* 16 (1 & 2), 1-20.

Sobel, D., & Klein, A. C. (1996). *Backache: What exercises work.* New York, NY: St. Martin's Griffin.

Takano, Y., & Osaka, E. (1999). An unsupported common view: Comparing Japan and the US on individualism-collectivism. *Asian Journal of Social Psychology,* 2, 311-341.

Turabian, K. L. (Revised by Grossman, J. & Bennett, A.) (1996). *A manual for writers of term papers, theses and dissertations* (6th ed.). Chicago, IL: The University of Chicago Press.

Van Leunen, M. C. (1992). *A handbook for scholars (rev. ed.).* New York, NY: Oxford University Press.

PART III

Writing the Research Paper

CHAPTER 5

Writing the Research Paper: Introduction, Body & Conclusion
論文の三要素

Aims :
1. To be able to write a good introduction.
2. To be able to write a good topic sentence.
3. To be able to write a good paragraph.
4. To be able to write a good conclusion.

　第1章から4章までは論文を書く前に必要な準備段階について説明してきた。第5章では、論文の「書き方」について解説していきたい。
　英語の論文は通常、簡単に分けると3つの部分で構成されている。それは introduction（序説）、body（本文）と conclusion（結論）である。この3つの部分はさらに、それぞれ幾つかの paragraph で構成されている。そして各 paragraph は幾つかの sentence で構成されている（Figure 5.1 を参照）。
　良い英語の論文を書くためには、各 introduction、body と conclusion が、論文全体の中でどのような役割を果たしているかについて理解することが大切である。特に論文全体の構成を紹介する introduction は、論文の良し悪しが一目瞭然となる部分であり、高い完成度が求められる。また、introduction、conclusion ともに、一定のスタイルに基づいて書くことが要求されるため、慎重な推敲が必要である。以下、詳しく解説したい。

☆ Figure 5.1: Components of a Paper

Introduction*

Xxxx xxx xxx xxxx xxxx xx x. X xxx xxx xxx x xxx xxx xx xx xxxxxx xxxxxx xxxxxxxxx xxxxxxxx xx. Xxxxxx xx x.
　Xx xxxxxxx xx xxxxxxx xxxxxxxxx xxxxxxxx xxxxxxxxxxxx xxxxx

Present Conditions of Women in Business*

Xxxx xxx xxx xxxx xxxxx xxx xx. Xxxx xxx xxxxxxxxx xxxx xxxx xxxx .
　Xxxxx xxxx xxxxx xxxx xxxx . Xxx xxxxx xxxx xxxxx xxxx xxxxxx xxxxxx xxxxxxxx xxxxxxxx xxxxx.

Causes of Gender-Inequality*

Xxxx xxx xxx xxxx xxxx xx x. X xxx xxx xxx x xxx xxx xx xx xxxxxxx.
　Xxxxxxxxx xxxxxxxxx xxxxxxxxx xxxx xx xxxxx xx xxxxxxx xx xxxxxxx xxxxxxxxx xxxxxxxx xxxxxxxxxxxx xxxxx

Some Possible Solutions*

Xxxx xxx xxx xxxx xxxx xx x. X xxx xxx xxx x xxx xxx xx xx xxxxxxx.
　Xxxxxx xx xxxxxxxxxxxx xxxxxxxxx xxxxxxxx xx xxxxxxxx xx xxxxxxx xxxxxxxxx xxxxxxxx xxxxxxxxxxxx xxxxx

Conclusion*

Xxxx xxx xxx xxxx xxxx xx x. X xxx xxx xxx x xxx xxx xxxx.
　Xxxxxx xx xxxxxxxxx xx xxxxxxxxx xxxxxxxxx xx xx xxxxxxx xx xxxxxx xxxxxxxxxxxxxx xxxxx.

*小見出し

5A Introduction
論文の書き出しについて

　Introduction は論文において、セールスマン的役割を果たしていると考えるとよい。あなたがある商品の電話セールスを行っているとしよう。相手が電話を切る前に商品の説明をすばやくしなくてはいけないとしたら、あなたは何から話していくだろうか。

　まずは相手の興味を引くことが大切である。いち早く興味を引かないと電話を切られるからだ。次にその商品の必要性について論じるかもしれない。さらに、あなたの会社の商品がどのように他社のものと違うかを説明し、最後にその商品の特徴などを簡単に説明するかもしれない。

　論文の introduction も同じである。研究者は多数ある論文の中からどれを最後まで読むかを決めるために introduction を読む場合が多い。そのためにも introduction には下記の4つの要素が必要だといわれている。

☆ **Figure 5.2**

Introduction の4つの要素

(i) 読み手の興味を引くもの。
↓
(ii) 論文の意図や重要性を示すのに効果的と思われる背景等の説明。
［同じ文章で (i) と (ii) 両方をカバーする場合もある。］
↓
(iii) Thesis statement として表わす論文の趣旨。Thesis statement は introduction の最後につける人が多い。
↓
(iv) 論文の構成の説明。
［同じ文章で (iii) と (iv) 両方を含んでいる場合もある。］
(Langan, 1985; Oshima & Hogue, 1991)

ここで Reading 1B の introduction を例にとり、その構成を分析してみよう。

> ★ **Figure 5.3: Analysis of Reading 1B's Introduction**

（ⅰ）読み手の興味を引くもの

（ⅱ）論文の意図や重要性を示すのに効果的と思われる背景等の説明

A fallacy of some repute and some duration is the one which assumes that because a student can write an adequate essay in his native language, he can necessarily write an adequate essay in a second language. (Kaplan, 1966, p. 3)

According to Kaplan (1966), many foreign students with advanced English proficiency have been told by their instructors that their papers are "somehow out of focus," "lack organization," or "lack cohesion." In other words, their papers do not appear "logical" to their instructors. If these same students are able to write "well-organized" and "logical" papers in their native language, it would seem only natural for them to be able to transfer this skill to their second language. What, then, is causing this problem? Some researchers (Kaplan, 1966; Okabe, 1993) argue that this is because the definition as well as purpose of "logic" and "rhetoric" vary across cultures. On the other hand, many studies have shown that the conventions that govern research articles have become universal. For example, Taylor & Chen (1991) comparing Anglo-American and Chinese scientific texts found that the underlying patterns take "virtually no account of language systems, and little account of either national or disciplinary culture" (p. 332). In our increasingly interdependent world, perhaps the standards that govern "good academic writing" have become universal. However, the fact remains that knowledge of the English language is not enough. To write a "good paper" in English, one must understand the definition, components and purposes of a "research paper." This reading passage will, therefore, begin by presenting a definition of a "research paper," followed by a summary of the characteristics of an "effective paper" as presented by Langan (1985).

（ⅲ）Thesis statement として表わす論文の趣旨。Thesis statement は introduction の構成の説明の前につける人が多い

（ⅳ）論文の構成の説明

Reading 1B の thesis は「英語で良い論文を書くにはまず論文における『良さ』とは何か、また何を目標に論文を書くのかを把握する必要がある」ということである。ただ、この主張をいきなり何の前触れもなく書いては読み手の興味を引くことができない。(i) そこでこの introduction はまず「多くの人は母国語で論文が書ければ第二外国語でも当然書けるだろう、という誤った知識を持っている」という他の研究者の言葉の引用（quote）で始めている。(ii) さらに論文の thesis の重要性をより明確にするために、「英語がかなりできる学生でもなぜかレポートは論理的ではない、しっくりこない等といわれるケースが多い」ということを述べている。(iii) 次にその現象の原因としては色々考えられるがとりあえず「英語で良い論文を書くことは論文の定義や目的等を把握するところから始まる」という thesis にたどりついている。(iv) 最後に、その thesis を論証するために、この後展開されることになる論文の構成と趣旨の展開のあらましが説明されている。

🔒 Exercise 5A-1:　Introduction の 4 つの要素

　次の 3 つの introduction を読み、（ ）の後の sentence は、Figure 5.2 で説明した要素 i ～ iv のどれに当たるかを（ ）に記入しなさい。

1. （　）Despite the women's liberation movement and the implementation of E.E.O. (Equal Employment Opportunity),[1] women are still far from being equal partners to men in business. （　）A 1990 study by Mary Ann Von Glinow of the University of Southern California revealed that, in the top Fortune 500 companies, a mere 2.6% of corporate executives (vice presidential level and higher) were occupied by women. （　）Corporations need to reexamine their hiring and promoting practices to investigate what is causing this inequality. （　）This paper will begin by first exploring the present conditions of women in business, proceed by analyzing the causes

---

1　E.E.O. - 雇用機会均等法

of gender-inequality, and conclude by recommending some possible solutions.

2.   ( ) A-23-year old female returnee who lived in the U.S.A. between the ages of 10 to 15 and again from 18 to 22 . . . returned to Japan last year. . . according to her, the most shocking thing was to be treated as though there was something "deficient" about her. Considering her background, it makes sense that she is more proficient in English than Japanese. She claims, however, to have been called a cripple by other Japanese. Initially she had problems getting along with other Japanese and thus tried very hard to please everyone around her. As a result, she ended up feeling depressed because she didn't feel like she was herself anymore. On the surface she looks well-adjusted and very "Japanese." Inside, however, she continues to struggle with this conflict. (Hoshino, 1986, p. 14, translation by the author)

( ) Many people feel that returnees nowadays are a privileged group who have the advantage of entering elite universities and companies due to their language skills. Although this may be true to a certain extent, societal pressures to act "Japanese" often bring forth complex identity issues for these returnees (Enloe & Lewin, 1987; Horoiwa, 1986; Takahagi, 1982). ( ) If we are to help returnees take advantage of their unique experiences abroad, we need to help them resolve these issues. For returnees to become truly comfortable with their identity as multicultural individuals, however, society needs to change as well. ( ) This paper will begin by describing identity issues experienced by returnees and offer a model returnees can use to help them overcome the identity issues they are facing. Finally, society's role will be discussed and concrete suggestions will be offered.

3.   ( )What I hear, I forget,
　　　　What I see, I remember,
　　　　What I do, I understand.
　　　　(Confucius[2] 451 B.C.)

　For centuries, it has been common knowledge that "true" learning occurs from "doing." For example, traditionally children learned skills such as weaving, cooking, fishing or hunting not by attending lectures but by watching and helping their elders perform the activities. ( ) Unfortunately, most of the formal education we take part in nowadays focuses on "listening" to lectures and "reading" textbooks without much "doing." ( ) For "effective" learning to occur, lectures and reading assignments need to be followed up with assignments that require students to use the knowledge and skills acquired. ( ) This paper will begin by first introducing recent research supporting the importance of having students actively participate in the learning process. The ratio of "hearing" to "seeing," and "doing" in an average university course will then be presented. Finally, specific ways in which "doing" can be incorporated into the classroom setting will be introduced.

(i) 読み手の興味を引くもの

　論文の重要性を伝えながら読み手の興味を引くには色々な方法があるが、ここでいくつか主なものをあげてみよう。
　　a. 統計等を用いる。
　　b. Quote（格言）等を用いる。
　　c. 実話や case study（実例）等をあげる。

2　Confucius - 孔子

Exercise 5A-2: Introduction - (i) 読み手の興味を引くもの

　Exercise 5A-1 で (i)（読み手の興味を引くもの）と分類したものをさらに分析し、上記 a〜c の中のどのタイプなのか答えなさい。

読み手の興味を引く時に注意する点：

　日本人の学生の多くは、読み手の興味を引くために個人的なエピソードを用いる傾向がある。例えば、「春休みの間に初めてイギリスでホームステイを経験した。その時に……」等と。日本語のエッセイ調の文章だとよく使われる手法だが、英語の論文だと幼稚な印象を与えてしまう。第1章でも述べたように、レトリックは文化によって異なるからだ。岡部（1993）によると、論理性で説得する西欧的レトリックに比べ、日本的レトリックというのは「人間関係の調和の上になった感得をカギ概念とする」(p.78)。すなわち、聞き手または読み手との間に良い関係を築くようにして説得しようとする傾向がある。確かに日本語で書かれている本、特にエッセイ調の本を読んでいると、まるで作者の友人になったような気分になる。そして作者に好感を持つことにより、説得されてしまう。だが、なぜか同じことを英語の論文でやろうとすると主観的で子供っぽい印象になりがちである。

　なるべく主観的な印象を避けるためには次の3つを意識するとよい。

- "I"という一人称単数代名詞をなるべく避けるようにする。[3] 論題がどのように自分一人に関係するのかではなく、どのように社会全般に影響を及ぼすかなどと、一般論化した説明をするためである。
- 統計や研究結果等、客観的な情報を使う。
- 実例等もケーススタディー（実例研究）形式でなるべく三人称で語る。

3　I を絶対に使ってはいけない、というルールはないし、実際の論文をみても I を使っているケースはたくさんある。ただし、その用法を熟知していないとひとりよがりで客観性を欠いた論文にみえがちなので、初めのうちは避けた方が無難である。ただし、分野や国によって "I" の使用に対してのルールが違うため、各自の分野のルールに従うように。

🔓 Exercise 5A-3: Introduction - (i) 読み手の興味を引くもの

次にあげる 1 ～ 5 の文例はかなり主観的な内容である。これと同じ内容を一般論化、もしくは客観化した文例は a ～ e のどれに当たるか（ ）に記入しなさい。また 1 ～ 5 が a ～ e とどのように違うのかを分析しなさい。

(　) 1. This morning, as I was reading the newspaper, I came across an article discussing the problem of bullying[4]...

(　) 2. Every time I go to the supermarket, I am shocked at the amount of excess wrapping used...

(　) 3. This past summer, I went to Australia and stayed with an Australian family for two months. Strangely enough, I learned how "Japanese" I was through this experience...

(　) 4. Recently, several of my friends got divorced. I have also noticed that many recent TV dramas feature main characters who are divorced...

(　) 5. When I was a little boy, I remember my mother telling me not to cry because I was a boy...

---

a. As culture is so much a part of our lives, we are often unaware of its influence until we encounter another（Brislin, 2008）.

b. Most Japanese boys grow up being told not to cry because they are boys（Vitelli, 2013）.

4　bullying - いじめ

c. Divorce has recently become a common occurrence in Japan. According to the Statistical Handbook of Japan (2014), the divorce rate in Japan has incresced steadily since the 1960s...

d. A trip to a Japanese supermarket can be a shocking experience for the environmentally conscious person（Milroy-Maher, 2014）.

e. Although bullying has been acknowledged as a serious problem in Japan for many years, suicides by victims of bullying are still a common occurrence（Murai, 2015）.

Exercise 5A-4:　Introduction - (i) 読み手の興味を引くもの

次の 1 ～ 5 の主観的な印象を与えると思われがちな文例を読み、それを一般論化、もしくは客観化した文例に言い換えなさい。Exercise 5A-3 を参照するように。

1. This morning, as I was reading the newspaper, I came across an editorial discussing government officials receiving bribes from businesses...

   _____
   _____

2. Every time I go into a freezing cold office building in the summer, I am shocked at the extravagant waste of electricity...

   _____
   _____

3. Through my experience raising two children, I know that being a "mother" is a full-time job. Strangely enough, mothers do not receive any salaries, paid vacations, nor other benefits associated with a full-time job...

   _____
   _____

4. Recently, I have noticed many more non-Japanese living in Japan. Being in Hiroo or Roppongi almost gives the impression of being in a foreign country...

   _____
   _____

5. Ever since I was a child, I remember being told repeatedly by everyone how important it is to enter a good university...

   _____
   _____
   _____

(ii) 論文の意図や重要性を示すのに効果的と思われる背景等の説明

　上記の例を見てもわかるように (i) 読み手の興味を引きながら、同時に (ii) 論文の意図や重要性を示すのに効果的と思われる背景等の説明をする場合がある。そうでない場合は、(ii) を別の文章として書く必要がある。背景説明に便利な表現を幾つかここで紹介する。

Useful Expressions 5A:

- It is widely recognized that . . .
- For a number of years now, the role of ___ has been of interest and concern to . . .
- ___ have long been of interest to scholars and practitioners . . .
- Research indicates that . . .
- In early ___ history, the . . .
- In recent years there has been a great deal of discussion concerning . . .
- Numerous researchers have proposed different perspectives in approaching . . .
- Throughout the 20th century . . .
- It is well documented that . . .
- Recent research has focused on . . .
- Recently, there has been considerable interest in . . .

Exercise 5A-5: Introduction - (ii) 論文の意図や重要性を示すのに効果的と思われる背景等の説明

Exercise 5A-3 の a ～ e（118 ～ 119ページ）の後につながるような (ii) 論文の意図や重要性を示すのに効果的と思われる背景等の説明を書きなさい。（ここでは論文構成の手法を学ぶのが目的なので正確な統計資料を使う必要はない。今回は、適当なデータを「創作」することを認めることとする。）また、上記の Useful Expressions 5A の表現を適宜、用いるように。ただし、a ～ e の中に、すでに背景の説明等が入っている場合、N/A (Not Applicable)[5] と記入しなさい。

5　N/A (Not Applicable) - 該当しない

a. _____

b. _____

c. _____

d. _____

e. _____

(iii) Thesis statement として表す論文の趣旨

(47 ～ 51 ページ参照)

(iv) 論文の構成の説明

　前述の通り、introduction は読み手の興味を引き、論文の意図や重要性を示すだけではなく、論文の構成を簡潔に説明する役目を果たしている。すなわち、introduction を読むだけで、論文の outline が推測できるはずである。論文の構成の説明は introduction の最後にあることが多い。

🔒 Exercise 5A-6: Introduction - (iv) 論文の構成の説明

　Exercise 5A-1（114〜116ページ）で取り上げた introduction を読み、論文の outline を推測しなさい。下記の1の例を参考に、2〜3について分析しなさい。

(例) **#1**　I. Introduction-Thesis: Corporations need to reexamine their hiring and promoting practices to investigate what is causing this inequality.
　　　　II. The present conditions of women in business
　　　　III. Causes of gender inequality
　　　　IV. Some possible solutions
　　　　V. Conclusion

#2　Thesis:

#3　Thesis:

📎 Useful Expressions 5A: Introduction - (iv) 論文の構成の説明

　以下に、構成の説明によく使われているパターンを6つあげる。a〜cのうち1つを選び、矢印に従って進むことで、論文の構成を説明することができる。なお / で区切られている2つからは、どちらか1つを選ぶこと。

1

　　　　　　　a This paper will begin by . . .
　　　　　　　a This paper first provides a . . .
　　　　　　　　　　↓

b Next, it will . . .**b** it will then proceed by . . .**b** the . . . will then be presented . . .**b** Following this review . . .
↓
c Finally, . . .**c** and conclude by . . .**c** Specifically, this paper discusses . . .

2

a (Thus,) one purpose in this chapter/article is . . .
↓
b A second purpose of this chapter/article (, therefore,) is . . .
↓
c A . . . also is presented.

3

a (Thus,) this article has two purposes.
↓
b The first is to . . .
↓
c The second purpose is to . . .

4

a In an attempt to . . . this study investigates . . .**a** The investigation of . . . involved two stages . . .
↓
b First, . . .**b** The first . . .
↓
c Next, . . .**c** The second . . .

5

a This paper describes . . . **a** The present paper focuses on . . . **a** <u>Our study/The present study explores the</u> . . . **a** This paper provides a . . .

6

a This discussion is organized around three topics: ___, ___ and ___.
　a The purpose of this paper is twofold. First ___. Second ___.

🔒 Exercise 5A-7:　Introduction - (iv) 論文の構成の説明

Exercise 5A-1 の 1 ～ 3 について「構成を説明する文」を書き換えてみよう。下記の 1 の例を参考に、2 ～ 3 について書いてみなさい。

（例）1. This paper first provides a brief overview of present conditions of women in business. Next, it will explore and analyze the causes of gender-inequality. Finally, it will recommend some possible solutions.

2. _____
_____
_____

3. _____
_____
_____

上級者向けのワンポイント

　この章では introduction の4つの要素について説明したが、実際に論文を書く際には全体のバランスを考えてほしい。人間の体でいうと introduction が頭、body が体で conclusion が足部だと考えてほしい。1ページくらいのエッセイの場合は introduction の4つの要素を全ていれる必要はない（iii と iv のみで十分である）。逆に20ページの論文の場合はもっと念入りに introduction を書く必要がある。例えば社会科学の学術誌の論文の introduction では4つの要素以外に、(ii) と (iii) の間あたりに、今までどのような研究がされてきて (e.g., "While...has been studied quite extensively...")、どの側面が不足していて (e.g., "few studies have examined...")、かつ現行の論文ではどのようにその穴を埋めるか (e.g., "This study seeks to fill this gap by...") を説明する場合が多い。

Applications 5A: Introduction

　ここで Applications 3B（69〜70ページ）で書いた outline を用い、このテキストで学習して書こうと思う論文の introduction を書き始めなさい。Introduction に必要な4つの要素（112ページを参照）を確認しながら書くように。実際に論文を書く際には Introduction をまずおおまかに書いておいて、本文執筆に合わせながら手直ししていく人もいる。また論文を書きあげてから、最後に introduction を書く人もいる。自分にとってもっともやりやすい方法を見つけるとよい。

5B Conclusion
論文の締めくくりについて

　論文を読んでいる読者は細かい議論にとらわれ、論文の趣旨を忘れがちになることがある。そのためにも conclusion でもう一度論文の趣旨、すなわち thesis を読者に伝える必要がある。ただし thesis を言い換えるだけでは introduction とあまり変わらない。実は conclusion にはもう1つ大事な役割がある。それは今後の課題等を提示することである。方法は色々ある。読み手に向かって考えさせる質問を投げかけたり、これから検討すべきことや、さらに調査すべき点や著者の研究の結果から予想できることを示し、アドバイスすることである。

☆ **Figure 5.4**

Conclusion の2つの要素
(i) 要点のまとめと、introduction で紹介した thesis の再度の強調。
↓
(ii) 読み手を考えさせる質問、これから検討すべきことや調査すべき点や著者の研究の結果、今後の展望、アドバイス等。
[同じ文章で (i) と (ii) 両方を含む場合もある。]
(Langan, 1985; Oshima & Hogue, 1991)

Useful Expressions 5B:

次のような表現を用いることにより、conclusion だということがより明確になる。[6]

In conclusion . . .	In summary . . .	To summarize . . .
In brief . . .	In sum . . .	To conclude . . .
Thus . . .		

Exercise 5B-1: Conclusion - (i) 要点のまとめ

次の1〜5の thesis statement を読み、conclusion の (i) の要素を組み込んで言い換えたものを、a〜e から選び、（ ）に記入しなさい。

( ) 1. Movies contain endless potential for teaching culture.

( ) 2. A close look at the traditional tea ceremony in Japan reveals many values that lie at the core of Japanese culture.

( ) 3. Life after retirement can be one of the most enjoyable times in one's life.

( ) 4. For effective recycling to occur, consumers need to actively purchase recycled goods.

( ) 5. Since people learn the most when they want to learn,

---

6 Exercise 5B-1 の a〜e の例を見てもわかるように、conclusion に必ずしもこうした型通りの phrase を使う必要はない。むしろ、こうした「型」を応用し、自分の論文にとってより効果的な文章を作る努力をすることが重要である。

motivation should be the criteria for entering a university, not age.

a. Thus, it cannot be overemphasized that recycling must begin with the consumers.

b. Since motivation is the key to true learning, there is no reason to set an age limit for studying at a university.

c. In sum, it can be said that understanding the tea ceremony is a step toward understanding Japanese culture.

d. After a lifetime of working, life after retirement can provide the much needed time and opportunity for individuals to do what they truly enjoy.

e. In sum, it can be said that selectively chosen movie excerpts are an effective way to teach culture and cultural differences.

Exercise 5B-2:　Conclusion - (i) 要点のまとめ

次の thesis statement を conclusion で使うために言い換えなさい。

a. When doing business across cultures, one may find a "perfectly appropriate gift" mistaken for a bribe.

b. Since human relationships are of utmost importance to many Japanese, apologies serve an important purpose in Japanese society.

c. Although Equal Employment Opportunity (E.E.O.) is required in Japanese companies, most places have invisible barriers that block women from being promoted to executive level positions.

🔒 Exercise 5B-3: Conclusion - (i) 要点のまとめ

Exercise 5A-1 (114～116ページ) の introduction を読み、それに基づいて conclusion を書きなさい。 その時に conclusion の2つの要素を組み込むことを忘れないように。(ここでは論文のまとめ方を学ぶのが目的なので正確な統計資料を使う必要はない。今回も、適当なデータを「創作」することを認めることとする。) スペースが不足なら別紙を用いなさい。

(例)

1. In conclusion, it can be said that gender equality in the workplace is not yet a reality. In fact, at the present rate, "true equality" will not be reached for another 475 years (England, 1992). As the U.S. Department of Labor's Glass Ceiling Commission's study has revealed, even if human resource policies appear to be "fair" on the surface, often many invisible barriers (glass ceilings), exist to prevent women from being promoted to upper level management positions. Corporations seeking to create a "truly equal" work environment must first begin by reexamining the glass ceilings that affect their hiring and promoting practices.

2. _____

3. _____

> **上級者向けのワンポイント**

　社会科学の学術論文などでは、conclusion では、自分の論文がどのような貢献をしているかを強調するために、今回の研究結果がどのように理論 (Ramifications for Theory)、研究方法論 (Ramifications for Research)、そして実践の場 (Ramifications for Practice) に影響を与えるのかを詳しく論じていくと良い。また、紹介している研究の limitations（限界）と今後の課題をなるべく沢山あげることで、その分野の発展を促進できるだろう。

5C Body
論文の本文を効果的に表現するには

Body

　論文の概要を知るため、読者は introduction、そして各 paragraph の最初の sentence、最後に conclusion を読むことが多い（111 ページの Figure 5.1 の楕円で囲った部分を参照）。Introduction と conclusion では論文の趣旨や構成を説明し、これからの展望を紹介しているからであり、また各 paragraph の論旨を伝えるための topic sentence が paragraph の冒頭にあるからだ。すなわち、introduction、各 paragraph の topic sentence と conclusion により論文の outline がわかるのが良い論文といえる。

Paragraph

　各 paragraph の topic sentence に続く文章を supporting sentences といい、topic sentence を展開し、具体的な例を挙げたり、詳しく述べたり、

広げたりする役割を果たしている。そして、paragraph の最後には簡単なまとめ等が入る。すなわち、paragraph そのものもある程度自己完結しているものである（Figure 5.5 を参照）。

　Topic sentence は thesis statement と同様、漠然とテーマを紹介するだけではなく、方向性を表わす必要がある。

☆ **Figure 5.5**

Paragraph の 3 つの要素

(i) Topic Sentence
↓
(ii) Supporting Sentences
(Topic sentence を展開し、統計を紹介したり、
具体的な例を挙げたり、詳しく述べたり、広げたりする)
↓
(iii) Concluding Sentence(s) ←必要に応じて
(Arnaudet & Barrett, 1981; Oshima & Hogue, 1991)

ここで次の paragraph を分析してみよう。

[Topic Sentence] [詳しく述べている]

A good topic is one that is specific enough for you to cover within the prescribed amount of space. If your topic is too big, your paper will probably be shallow and uninteresting. Your topic should also be one that you are interested in and knowledgeable about. If you are interested and knowledgeable about your topic, you will be more motivated to write about it, making it more interesting for the audience as well (Shaw, 1984).

[広げている] [詳しく述べている]

まず、冒頭のtopic sentenceでは「良いトピックとは与えられている字数内で書けるくらいに絞ったものである」と主張している。次のセンテンスではその主張をサポートするために、トピックを絞らないとどうなるかについて説明している。そこから話を広げ、次のセンテンスでは「トピックは自分が興味があるうえ、知識のある分野であるべきだ」と説明している。そして、最後のセンテンスではそれをさらに詳しく述べている。

Exercise 5C-1: Paragraphs

Reading 2B（34ページ～）、3B（62ページ～）と4B（80ページ～）に戻り、各paragraphのtopic sentenceを○で囲みなさい。次に、supporting sentencesの役割（topic sentenceを展開したり、具体的な例を挙げたり、詳しく述べたり、広げたりする）を書き込みなさい。Concluding sentence等がはっきりとある場合はそれも表示しなさい。次の Reading 4A の例を参照しなさい。Topic sentence は paragraph の冒頭にあることが多いが、必ずしもそうではないので注意すること。

Reading 4A Conducting a Literature Review

Once you have a general idea of what you plan to write about, it is time to go to the library to conduct a literature review. A literature review serves two main purposes. First of all, it will reveal to you how much, if any, research has already been done on your topic. You will learn what kinds of studies have already been carried out as well as the results of those studies. Secondly, it will provide you with concrete evidence to support your thesis. Here, let us examine three main ways in which to conduct a literature review: (1) using online library catalogs, (2) using computer databases, and (3) using the reference lists found at the end of articles and books.

―[Introduction]

The library catalog is useful in locating books that are available within a particular library system. For example, the National Diet Library has its own library catalog called the 国立国会図書館サーチ (http://iss.ndl.go.jp/). This can be used to locate books available at their library as well as other public libraries around Japan. Using their "Advanced search" (詳細検索) option, you can conduct your search based on the Title (タイトル) or Author・Editor (著者・編者). If you do not have a particular book in mind, doing a subject (件名) search is probably best.

Once you have a list of books to look for, you are ready to go to the bookshelves. At the bookshelves, instead of simply taking the books on your list and leaving, take a moment to look around the bookshelves where you found the books. You may be pleasantly surprised to find other books that, for one reason or another, did not show up during your initial search.

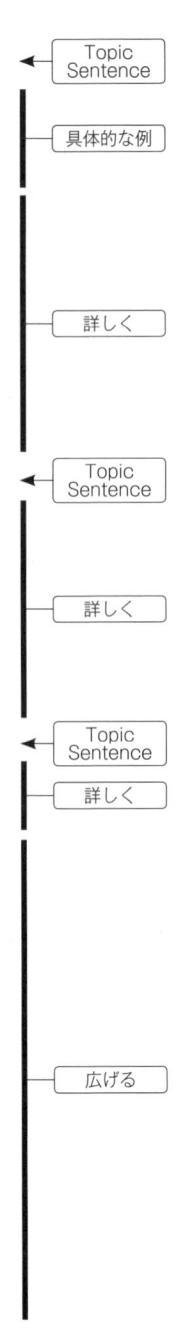

The library database is the best way to locate journal articles. Since articles take less time to publish than books, the most recent findings tend to be published as articles before they become books. EBSCO HOST is useful for locating English journal articles while CiNii (http://ci.nii.ac.jp/) is convenient for Japanese ones. Both databases will provide PDF versions of the articles, when available, for immediate download. If a PDF version is not available the library database will often provide options for tracking down the article in your own or nearby library. If the article is not available through your local library system or if you need help locating sources, consult a reference librarian. Today, an increasing number of journal articles can be found online so using a search engine such as Google or Google Scholar can augment what you have already found. When using such general search engines make sure that the article is coming from a reputable journal, magazine, or newspaper, not just someone's webpage, blog or Wikipedia.

After finding relevant books or articles, always look at the "reference list" found at the back of the document to see if there are any other publications that look interesting. Again, you may be pleasantly surprised to find sources that you missed during your initial search.

To access a wide variety of materials, you should not limit your search to English materials. It is not only acceptable but is actually preferable to include materials written in Japanese as well as other languages in which you may be proficient. If you wish to publish your article in an English language journal, your ability to cite studies written in Japanese or other languages will give you an edge over others who can only read English. Journal editors will be more likely to accept your article because it provides references and information that might not have been previously published in English.

Depending on your topic, some of you may find only a few sources. Others may find that it is an unending process. Each article or book leads to several more, which lead to more and so on and so forth. Ideally, a literature review is conducted until there is no more to be found. Realistically, however, the amount of time as well as the limited availability of resources will inevitably limit your search.

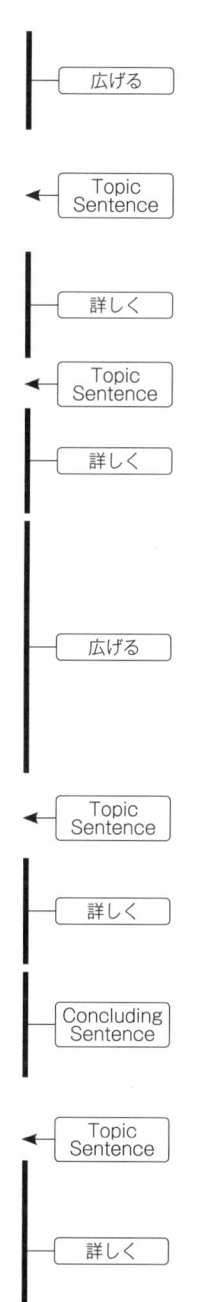

What you have found through your literature review should be valuable not only for the research paper you are working on but for future papers as well. For that reason, it is important to keep copies of documents and to file them in an orderly fashion. Make sure to label all the copies with the author's name, title, date, name of journal, name of publisher, as well as other pertinent information so that if you quote it in your paper you can cite it correctly in the reference list.

詳しく

Conducting a literature review is, perhaps, the most exciting as well as the most time consuming part of working on your research paper. A comprehensive literature review will not only provide you with sufficient background information on your topic but will also give you concrete evidence to use in supporting your thesis statement.

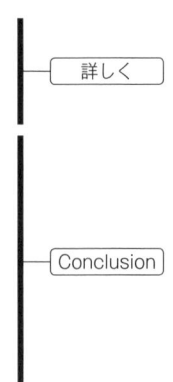

Conclusion

Exercise 5C-2: Organizing Paragraphs

次の文章を並べ替え、論旨の明確なパラグラフを完成させなさい。答えは下線の上に書くように（例：A，C，B，D）。1番と2番はあらかじめtopic sentenceが与えられている。

1. Topic Sentence: While it is true that many people work for money, work provides us with much more than money.
    A) Their identity, as a mother, is taken away from them with nothing to replace this empty hole.
    B) One solution would be for companies to make it easier for working women to raise children while they work.
    C) For many of us it provides us with an identity. For example, when people ask us what we do, we tend to answer that question by telling them our profession.
    D) Another solution would be for companies to provide many job opportunities for women who wish to return to the workplace.
    E) This is why many women who quit their jobs to raise their children sometimes face an identity crisis, especially after their children have grown up.

Answer: _____

2. Topic Sentence: While hard work is clearly essential for success, luck also plays an important role.
   A) I acknowledge that I do work hard and that hard work should be rewarded. However, I also believe that success in life is often a combination of luck and hard work.
   B) My subsequent jobs were both introduced to me by an alumnus of my university. If I had not gotten to know her during university, I would not have known about these positions.
   C) I heard about an opening for a position at my first place of employment through my advisor in graduate school. Had I studied at a different school or under a different advisor, I would not have known about that job.
   D) For example, all three of the jobs that I have held, were acquired not only through hard work but through luck and timing.
   E) These examples illustrate, that at least for me, hard work and luck have both played an important role in my success.

   Answer: _____

3.
   A) As exercise and a healthy diet are both essential to our health, schools should not only provide physical education classes but also other opportunities for students to exercise.
   B) This is especially important today, when "play" for most children consists of a solitary activity involving game consoles. Schools should also teach them how to live a long and healthy life.
   C) Schools should not simply teach students academics but should also provide them with other kinds of education. For example, schools should teach children how to interact with their peers

and other adults.

D) In sum, to provide children with a well-rounded education, schools must, therefore, teach not only academics but also provide many possible ways in which a child can grow.

Answer: _____

4.

A) Alternatively, it could be caused by the lack of social interaction in our lives; humans might be seeking love and affection from pets instead of other human beings.

B) Everything from day care, hotels, hair salons, cafes, dance classes, and yoga are available for pets. Some people even host birthday parties and funerals for their beloved pets.

C) The pet industry is expanding rapidly these days.

D) This tendency to treat pets as family members could simply be a reflection of the relatively peaceful and affluent times in which we live.

E) In either case, it looks like the pet industry will continue to thrive for years to come.

Answer: _____

Applications 5C: Writing the Paper

論文の本文に着手しよう。

Writing for Fun 5: TOEFL Writing その1

この章では Introduction, Body, Conclusion について紹介してきた。学術論文に挑戦する前に、もっと短い TOEFL の Writing セクションのエッセイで、論文作成の練習をしてみよう。TOEFL の Writing セクションでは、最低でも 300 単語のエッセイを 30 分以内に書かなくてはいけない。トピックの例は Google で TOEFL Writing Topics で検索すれば出てくるので、あらかじめいろいろな問題で練習しておくとよい。TOEFL を受験する予定がない場合でも、エッセイの練習によいのでお勧めである。TOEFL 受験予定の場合、留意すべき点は（1）論理的であること、（2）なるべくたくさん書くこと、と（3）文法の誤りやスペルミスがないことである。なるべく簡単な文章を使い、誤りがないこと、である。

下記のトピックで 300 単語以上のエッセイを書いてみよう。(30 分以内を目安に仕上げること)。

If you were an employer, which kind of worker would you prefer to hire: an inexperienced worker at a lower salary or an experienced worker at a higher salary? Use specific reasons and details to support your answer.

最近では文法やスペリングを自動的にチェックしてくれるウェブサイトもあるので、模範例を見る前に自分の書いたものをチェックしてみよう。

http://www.paperrater.com/

References

Arnaudet, M. L., & Barrett, M. E. (1981). *Paragraph development: A guide for students of English as a second language.* Englewood Cliffs, NJ: Prentice Hall.

Brislin, R. (2008). *Working with cultural differences: Dealing effectively with diversity in the workplace.* Westport, CT: Praeger.

England, P. (1992). *Comparable work: Theories and evidence.* New York, NY: Aldine de Gruyter.

Enloe, W., & Lewin, P. (1987). Issues of integration abroad and readjustment to Japan of Japanese returnees. *International Journal of Intercultural Relations, 11,* 223-248.

Gardner, J. (1983). *On becoming a novelist.* New York, NY: Harper & Row.

Horoiwa, N. (1986). メタ的な生き方のすすめ [A recommendation toward living on the meta-level]. 教育と医学 *[Education and Medicine],* 10, 51 (957)-56 (962).

Hoshino, A. (1986). 異文化対処の失敗とカウンセリング [Failure to adapt to a new culture and counseling]. 教育と医学 *[Education and Medicine],10,* 12 (918)-21 (927).

Kaplan, R. B. (1966). Cultural thought patterns in intercultural education. *Language Learning: A Journal of Applied Linguistics, 16* (1 & 2), 1-20.

Langan, J. (1985). *College writing skills with readings.* New York, NY: McGraw-Hill Book Company.

Milroy-Maher, D. (2014, September 25). Japan has a dangerous fetish for packaging. *Vice.* Retrieved from http://www.vice.com

Murai, S. (2015, January 19). Bullying finds fertile ground in social media. *The Japan Times.* Retrieved from http://www.japantimes.co.jp

Okabe, R. (1993). 日本のレトリック [Japan's rhetoric]. In M. Hashimoto & S. Ishii. 日本人のコミュニケーション [*Japanese communication styles*] (pp. 55-81). Tokyo: Kirihara-shoten.

Oshima, A., & Hogue, A. (1991). *Writing academic English* (2nd ed.). Menlo Park, CA: Addison-Wesley Publishing Company.

Statistics Bureau, Management & Coordination Agency Government of Japan (総務庁統計局編). (1998). 第47回日本統計年鑑 [*Japan statistical yearbook*].

Takahagi, Y. et al. (1982). 海外／帰国子女におけるカルチャーショックの要因分析と適応プログラムの開発／施行 [An analysis of the causes of culture shock among returnees and the development and implementation of an adjustment program] No. 00445027. Tokyo: Tokyo Gakugei Daigaku Kaigai Shijo Kyouiku Center.

Vitelli, R. (2013, November 4). A crying shame: When is crying allowed in boys and girls? *Psychology Today.* Retrieved from https://www.psychologytoday.com

CHAPTER 6

Completing the Research Paper：論文を完成させるために

Aims：
1. To learn how not to give up in the middle of a research paper.
2. To understand the importance of proofreading and revising.
3. To learn how to proofread and revise.
4. To become aware of some frequently made mistakes by Japanese students.
5. To learn how to format a research paper.

6A Not Getting Discouraged
勇気をもって

　いざ論文を書き始めると、とてつもなく長い道のりに感じるかもしれない。練習問題をこなすたびに点数がつき、達成感があるのとは違い、論文は長時間かけてコツコツやるしかないからである。そのかわり最終的に仕上げた時の達成感は大きい。

　長い論文を書いている場合、途中でスランプに陥ることも多々あるだろう。人によってはなかなかエンジンがかからず、思い通り進まないかもしれない。気が付くと同じ sentence を何度も何度も書き直し、それでもしっくりこないこともある。

　小説家志望者の間ではなぜか 50 ページ書いた時点でやめたくなる現象があるといわれている。ちょうど人物紹介が終わり、話が始まるところでつまって

しまう。俗に "50-page syndrome"(Obstfeld, 1992) と呼ばれている。Obstfeld いわく、50 ページ書いてそのままになっている小説が世の中にあふれている、と。そのあふれている書きかけの小説と出版されている小説との大きな違いは、出版されている小説は最後まで書かれているということだ、と彼は主張している。終わらせたからといって必ず出版されるわけではないが、終わらせなければ絶対に出版される可能性はない。

　小説の場合と同じ現象が、論文を書いている人にもよく起こる。資料調べや調査が終わるまでは順調に進むが、なぜかそこで自分の研究に自信をなくし、止めてしまう。筆者もしばしば論文や本を半分くらい書き終えた時点で嫌気がさし、書きたくなくなることがある。その時励みになるのが筆者の恩師である Brislin 先生の言葉である。筆者が初めて本を執筆しようとしていた時に、Brislin 先生は Obstfeld と同じようなことを言ってくださった。「友子、出版できる人とできない人の一番の差は、出版できる人は最後まで原稿を書き終えることができるということだ。もし途中で自信をなくしても、とりあえず最後まで書き上げてみなさい」。確かに、そのまま使うか、捨てるかは原稿を書き上げてから決めても遅くないと自分に言い聞かせ、原稿を最後まで終わらせてきた。幸い、今のところ捨てた原稿は筆者にはない。

　小説家でもあり、大学で長年小説の書き方を教えていた John Gardner の次の言葉は新鮮に感じられる。"Originality is normally a quality achieved by diligence, not a natural condition" (Gardner, 1983, p. 134).

　小説も論文も書くのは大変なことである。膨大な時間と気力を要する、ということを覚悟のうえで取り組まなくてはいけない。途中であきらめず、最後まで小説を書き終えるために、Obstfeld (1992) は 5 つのヒントを提案している。その中から論文にも当てはまるものを筆者の経験とあわせて紹介していきたい。

◎ヒント１：いつ書くかを決めてそれを必ず守る
　筆者が教える立場にたち、学生の論文を読んでいて気が付くことは、良いものはそれなりに時間がかかっている、ということである。資料調べや構成を綿密に行い、rough draft を何度も revise したのがわかる。逆に良くない論文は、どうみても一夜漬けで書いたことがわかる。人間の心理なのかもしれない

が、だいたい英語に自信を持っている学生ほど時間をかけ、良いものを提出する。逆に英語に自信のない学生は論文を最後の最後まで放っておいて、徹夜で書いてしまう。それが成績に反映し、さらなる悪循環に陥っている。

　Obstfeld (1992) も提案しているが、1日にまとめて書かずに、コツコツと書き上げていくようなスケジュールをたてておくことが大切である。最低でも週に3回2時間ずつ論文に集中する時間を作る。できればいつも同じ時間帯に書くことが望ましい。その時間帯は電話の音声を消したりし、なるべく気の散ることがないようにする。人によっては1日のノルマを決める人もいる。本の執筆をしている場合は1日1〜2ページ位の人から8ページ（プロの中でもまれであるが）の人までいる。先に述べた筆者の恩師の Brislin 先生は1日2ページを目安に毎日午前7時から11時まで研究室のドアを閉めてひたすらコンピューターに向かっていた。一夜漬けに慣れていた筆者が初めてそれを聞いた時は「たったの2ページ！」と密かに思ったことをよく覚えている。その時 Brislin 先生は筆者の気持ちを察したのか、こうおっしゃった。「1日2ページって少なく感じるかもしれないが、1日2ページを週5日として月40ページだ。平均的な本はだいたい200ページだとするとだいたい5カ月で1冊書き終えることになる」と。当たり前だが、書いたものは全部使えるわけではない。読み返しているうちに削ったり、書き直したりするが、それでも Brislin 先生は平均して年に1〜2冊は本を出版していることを筆者は知っている。

◎ヒント2：スケジュールをたてる

　論文の場合、書くまでの時間が長い。特に大学の授業で課されるような論文はだいたい5〜8ページ位であり、実際に書く作業は1〜2週間みれば十分であるのに対し、執筆の準備と書き上げた草稿の推敲にはもっと長い時間がかかるはずだ。完成目標日に合わせて逆算しながら、いつまでに何をする、といったスケジュールをたてるとよい（Figure 6.1 を参照）。これまで各章の Applications を地道にこなしてさえいれば、今回の論文に関しての準備は順調に進んでいるはずなので、改めてスケジュールをたてる必要はないかもしれないが、今後、別の論文を書く場合、特に卒業論文等長いものを手がける時は、スケジュール表が必要となるだろう。

> ☆ **Figure 6.1：5ページの論文の場合のスケジュール表の例**

作業	スケジュール
トピックを絞る*	10月29日～11月2日
brainstorming/mindmapping をする*	10月29日～11月2日　(約5日)
thesis を決める*	10月29日～11月2日
資料を探す	11月4日～6日（約3日）
資料を読みながらノートをとる**	11月7日～14日（約8日）
構成を考えなおしながら outline を書く	11月15日～16日（約2日）
論文の rough draft を書きあげる	11月16日～25日（約10日）
自分で proofreading と revising をする	11月26日～30日（約5日）
他人に proofreading してもらう	12月1日～5日（約5日）
final draft を書き上げる	12月6日～7日（約2日）

*　この3つのプロセスは互いに影響しあうので、同時に行う人が多い。
**　実験や調査などをする場合は、その内容によってさらに数週間から数カ月まで余裕を見る必要がある。

◎ヒント3：集中する

よくある現象として「論文を書かなくては」と思い、座った瞬間、他の用事を思い出す、ということがある。例えば、今まで無視していた押し入れの整理整頓や冷蔵庫の掃除が、とたんに気になってきたり、どうしても机の上や本棚のほこりを拭かなくてはいけない気がしてくるものだ。そのような誘惑に負けずに書くことに集中できれば、それに越したことはないが、時と場合によっては雑用をやっている間に、頭がすっきりし、ものを書く意欲がわく可能性もある。ミステリー作家として有名な Agatha Christie も "The best time for planning a book is while you're doing the dishes"[1] (as cited in

---

1　do the dishes - 皿を洗う

Charlton, 1997, p. 93）と述べている。机に向かっている時に一番仕事がはかどるとは限らない。お風呂につかったり、散歩したり、泳いだりしている時の方が良いアイディアを思いつく人もいる。実際に書く作業も、家でするのが一番効率的だとは限らない。電車の中や喫茶店、公園や図書館の方が集中できるという人もいる。

◎ヒント４：人とのふれあいを大事にする

　ひとりでひたすら書いていると、自信ややる気をなくしがちである。第４章でも簡単に紹介したが、勉強会等でお互いの論文を読み、アドバイス等をしあう機会を作るようにすると励みになる。勉強会では論文の内容などを相談しあうことで、意外な意見やアドバイスをもらえるかもしれない。また、他の人の論文の中にも自分の論文に使える資料やアイディアを発見できるかもしれない。

　それ以外にも勉強会を通して他の人と苦しみや喜びを共有すると共に、ライバルとして競い合うことも大切である。他の人が一歩先に進むと、こっちもやる気になるものである。

◎ヒント５：先入観にとらわれない

　どうしてもある部分でつまずいてしまう場合は、その部分を飛ばして後で書く方が効率がよいこともある。Introduction は最初に書く、等という先入観にとらわれずに、書きやすいところを書きやすい時に書くとよい。人によっては本文をまず書いてから introduction を書くのを好むようである。筆者はよく、他の部分を書いている間に突然違うところについてひらめくことがある。そういう場合は忘れないうちにすぐにメモしておく。その時はちゃんとした文章で書かなくても、後でわかる程度にキーワード等を幾つか書いておけばよい。例えば「ここで例をあげる」「バーンランドの研究をここで紹介する」などと、書き留めておく。紙に書いた場合は付せん紙等をつけ、コンピューターの場合は太文字にしておき、まだ終わってないことを表示する。後からその部分だけをもう一度読みなおし、調べる必要のあるところを調べながら、ちゃんとした文章にしていく。

　論文の場合、実際の研究や他の文献等に基づいて書く部分が多いので、せっかく波にのって書いているのに一旦止めて資料を調べなくてはならないことに

なる。その間にせっかくの波をのがしてしまうこともある。書きながらあの研究をこの辺で使おうなどと考えたら、具体的な数字などは思い出せなくてもその場ですぐ資料を調べたりせず、後で調べられるように（　　）の中に「後で調べる」「統計を探す」「Langan の本を参照」等と自分に対してメモを書いておくとよい。

例えば：

"According to _____'s study (統計を調べる), ??% of the returnees surveyed reported some degree of reverse culture shock upon return to Japan." 等と書いておき、後で他のものと一緒にまとめて調べるとよい。

◎ヒント6：とにかく書く

Compose first, worry later. (Ned Rorem as cited in Charlton, 1997, p.76)

I write a lot — every day, seven days a week — and I throw a lot away. Sometimes I think I write to throw away; it's a process of distillation. (Donald Barthelme as cited in Charlton, 1997, p. 56)

訂正や変更は後から幾らでもできるのだから、とりあえず書いている間はあまり読み返さず、ひたすら書くことが肝心である。筆者もよく「こんなものでいいのかなあ」と思いつつ書くが、時間を少し置いてから読み返すと、思ったより良いこともある。気にいらないところは書き直せばよいので、とりあえず書くことにしている。読み返しはある程度切りのよいところまでまとまってからにしている。例えば各章が終わった時点や「今日はこれ以上書けない」と思った所などで行う。

論文の、とりあえず書き終えたものを rough draft という。その rough draft はあくまでも叩き台なので、それを書き直したり、足したり、削ったり、並び替えたりすることによって、より良いものにする。人によっては rough draft を書き上げた段階で力尽きてしまい、そのまま提出するが、それではまだ宝石に磨き上げられていない原石と同じである。

6B Proofreading & Revising
見直しと書き直しについて

　小説家はよく本を書くのを出産と子育てにたとえる、と Bryant (1992)は述べている。本を企画して構成し、rough draft を書くまでの段階は妊娠と出産のようで、苦しかったり、うれしかったりで、感動でいっぱいだという。逆に一通りできたものを何度も何度も読み返し、構成を変えたり、書き直したりするのは子供を大人になるまで育てる過程に似ているという。長時間にわたる地味な重労働だからだ。筆者の場合は rough draft ができて、ある程度形ができているものを「ああでもない、こうでもない」といじるのが逆に好きであるが、どちらにしろ、一通り書き上げてからもかなり時間がかかるという事実に変わりはない。読み直しをして、チェックをいれることを proofreading（または proofing）、そして訂正する過程を revising という。

　どういう形で proofreading や revising をするかは人によって違うが、筆者の場合を紹介しよう。筆者は直接コンピューターに打ち込むので、書き上げた段階でまずスペルチェックを行う。MS Word を使っている場合、スペルミスは赤文字で、文法ミスは緑で出てくるので、それを参照するとよい。右クリックするだけで訂正候補が出てくるので助かる。この機能を使うことで大体のスペリングミスが解決できる。なぜ「大体」かというと、コンピュータによるスペルチェックは、存在している言葉だったら何でも正しいと認識してしまうので、実際に存在しているが、使い方を間違えた言葉に関しては、間違いを見付け出すことができないからだ。例えば"of" を間違えて"if"と打ったり"and" のかわりに "an" と打った場合である。スペルチェックを終えたらドキュメント全体を印刷する。コンピューター画面上で proofreading や revising ができる人もいるが、筆者の場合、なぜか紙に印刷されたものの方がミスを見付けやすい。

　印刷されたものを初めから最後まで読み、変更したい部分をペン等で記入していく。一通り proofreading ができたら訂正をコンピューターに打ち込み、印刷する。そこでまた proofreading し revising を行う。何度かこうした作業を繰り返した時点で、原稿を何人かの友人等に読んでもらい、わかりにくい部分等を指摘してもらう。他人に読んでもらうことによって、原稿を新

たな視点から見直すことができ、大変参考になる。筆者の場合、数人の人にproofreading を依頼する。そこでまた訂正をコンピューターに入力し、印刷しておく。時間の余裕がある時はそのまま数日置いてからまた読み返すと、新鮮な見方ができる。前述の通り、rough draft はあくまでも叩き台なので、変えることに抵抗を感じてはいけない。筆者の場合、数ケ月かけて集めたデータを論文にまとめるのに、集中して書いても数週間から１ケ月くらいかかる。それを友人に読んでもらい、書き直すのにさらに２〜３ケ月はかかる。

　Proofreading には大きく分けて２種類あると考えてよい。まずは、内容面（content）である。Reading 1B で紹介した良い論文の４つの特徴のうちの最初の３つを意識するとよい。すなわち：
1. Advance a single point (thesis) and stick to that point.
2. Support the point with specific evidence.
3. Organize and connect the specific evidence.

　次に文法やスペリング等（mechanics）の細かい点である。ここでは良い論文の４つ目の特徴を意識するとよい（write clear, error-free sentences）。順序としては全体的な構成など内容面（content）をチェックしてから文法やスペリング等をチェックすると効率がよい。なぜかというと先に細かい所に時間をかけても、全体的な構成を考えた結果、その部分は省くべきだという結論に至る可能性があるからである。
　授業内レポートの場合は担当教員の基準に沿ってレポートを準備するとよい。参考までに筆者が学生に配るチェック・リストをこちらで紹介する。

Academic Paper Checklist

General checkpoints:
☐ Is my paper organized in a logical fashion?
☐ Do I have a clear thesis and did I stick to that point?
☐ Did I organize and connect the evidence to support my thesis?
☐ Did I write clear and error-free sentences?

Specific checkpoints:

☐ Have I included the FOUR components of an introduction?
☐ Have I included the TWO component of a conclusion?
☐ Does each paragraph have a topic sentence?
☐ Did I use headings and subheadings?
　Example:
　Introduction
　Background
　Conclusion
☐ Did I cite all my outside sources using the APA style?
　Example:
　Johnson (1999) argues…
　Research has found that… (Aimes, 2004)
☐ Did I paraphrase everything in my own words unless they are in quotation marks? (In other words, did I make sure that I did not plagiarize?)
☐ Is my reference list formatted according to the APA manual?
☐ Did I proofread my paper at least twice?
☐ Did I go over the list of "frequently made mistakes" (pp. 156-164) to make sure that I did not make those mistakes?
☐ Did I use the spell checker?
☐ Did I use the grammar checker?

　学術誌に投稿する場合は、必ず投稿規定に沿って準備すること。英語が母国語ではない場合は必ずネイティブ・チェックを依頼すること。また学術誌によってスタイルが異なるため、投稿する学術誌に記載されている論文をなるべくたくさん読み、その学術誌にあったスタイルに沿って論文を準備するとよい。先行研究に関しても、投稿する学術誌に掲載された関連論文はなるべく沢山参考にし、引用すると良い。

　ここから proofreading の練習を行おう。

Exercise 6B-1: Shortening Long Sentences

下記の長くて分かりにくい文章を、簡潔な文章に分けて書き直しなさい。一つのsentenceで一つのideaを表現することを基本として、内容を詰め込みすぎないように注意すること。

1. In the 1970s, when Japanese companies first started sending large numbers of employees abroad, returnee "problems" surfaced (Japan Overseas Educational Services, 1991) and children who grew up outside of Japan would return only to find that they could not adapt to schools in Japan and could not get into high schools or universities (Japan Overseas Educational Services, 1991).

2. Throughout history, there have been various methods of studying culture with psychologists typically take a micro-approach to cultural study, while sociologists analyze culture through more of a macro lens.

3. School Inspections are an important part of education in England and one of the researchers, who observed part of a three-day workshop designed for school managers given over the course of several weeks, found the following about school inspections.

_____
_____
_____
_____
_____
_____
_____

4. Returnees differ in their overseas experience in terms of the country or countries they lived in, the type of schools they attended, the number of years they spent abroad and their exposure to local culture but despite this variation, some generalizations have been made regarding interpersonal problems most commonly experienced by returnees.

_____
_____
_____
_____
_____
_____
_____

5. Over the course of their educational tenure, students are presented with a myriad of approaches that seek to improve their overall educational experience and the traditional teacher–student relationship has been supplemented with new modes of education that aim to create opportunities for improved student outcomes (e.g., Lewis et al., 2007; Shameem & Tickoo, 1999; Short, 1999).

6. Fantini (1995) points out that too often language teachers neglect teaching culture while interculturalists downplay the importance of language, he also argues that language and culture go hand in hand, each influencing the other.

7. Often students at large universities feel at a loss and lack a sense of belonging so Learning Communities create a medium through which they can engage in social interaction with individuals who have similar goals and can work cooperatively with them to attain those goals.

8. Not only is social interaction an effective way to learn language, culture, and attain a new worldview, but it is also a powerful way to motivate students, and many studies in the field of Higher Education (e.g., Astin, 1984; Pascarella & Terenzini, 1980, 1991; Tinto, 1975, 1993, 1997) have revealed the importance of student involvement and integration in retaining students in colleges and universities.

9. Although Japan remained fairly closed to foreigners for many years, recently there has been an influx in the number of foreign permanent residents and compared to1975 when there were only 751,842 registered foreigners in Japan, by 2010, the number almost tripled to 2,134,151 (法務省, 2010) and with this increase has been an increase in international marriages (厚生労働省, 2004) and children who are biethnic.

10. With the world becoming more global, many individuals are finding themselves growing up in the interstices of cultures and some are born in their passport countries and later move to another country while others are born and raised outside of their passport countries (Schaetti, 1999); some maintain their original nationality while others do not.

Exercise 6B-2: Eliminating Redundancy and Economizing Words

　良い文章は簡潔で分かりやすい。同じ意味の言葉をいくつも使ったり、必要のない言葉を使うと文章が分かりにくくなる。次の文章1～10は、有名な格言に筆者が余計な言葉を足したものである。不必要な言葉を削除し、もとの格言に戻しなさい。

1. They can do anything because they think they can do anything.

2. Every well-known artist was first an amateur artist.

3. I believe that education is the most powerful weapon which you can use to change the world today.

4. I have learned that every student can learn, just not on the same day, or the same way as each other.

5. You should live as if you were to die tomorrow. And you should learn as if you were to live forever.

6. Tell me something and I will forget, teach it to me and I may remember, involve me in an activity and I will learn.

7. Do not forget small kindnesses people do for you and do not remember their small faults.

8. To climb steep hills requires one to start with a slow pace at first.

9. You should try not to become a man of great success but instead try to be a man of true value.

10. It is known that a wise man will make more opportunities than those he finds in front of him.

6C Frequently Made Mistakes
良い英語を書くために

　ここで日本人の学生のレポートでよく見受ける間違いを幾つかとりあげていきたい。大きく分けて3つに分類してみた。

1. Category A: But, and, so, because 等の接続詞で sentence を始めない

　これは日本人に限らずアメリカ人の学生もよく注意される点である。ただ、多くの本を読むとこのような接続詞で始まっている sentence が現実にたくさんある。確かに、こなれた文章を書く人の場合、わざと接続詞で sentence を始めることもあるが、論文等では避けたほうが無難である。

2. Category B: Word Choice

　ここでは日本人の学生が使いがちな誤った表現を幾つかピックアップした。

3. Category C: Grammar & Mechanics

　文法や spelling、そして punctuation 等でよく見るミスを幾つか紹介したい。

A

But, and, so, because 等の接続詞で sentence を始めない

Inappropriate for Formal Writing	Possible Alternatives
● But the economy shows no sign of improvement. ● But little has been done by the government to prevent bullying from occurring. ● But many groups made up of concerned parents have been working hard on this issue. ● But bullying still continues to be a serious problem.	● The economy, however, shows no sign of improvement. ● Unfortunately, little has been done by the government to prevent bullying from occurring. ● On the other hand, many groups made up of concerned parents have been working hard on this issue. ● Nonetheless, bullying still continues to be a serious problem.
● So the environment in which children are raised affects their academic performance. ● So, many companies are undertaking radical measures.	● The environment in which children are raised, therefore, affects their academic performance. ● As a result, many companies are undertaking radical measures. ● This is why many companies . . . ● For this reason many . . .

CHAP 6

Completing the Research Paper

157

• <u>And</u> this study has been replicated many times. • <u>And</u> Johnson (20xx) was able to replicate this study as well.	• This study has been replicated many times. • <u>In addition</u>, many researchers have been able to replicate this study. • <u>Furthermore</u>, Johnson (20xx) was able to replicate this study. • <u>In fact</u>, Johnson (20xx) was able to replicate this study. • <u>Additionally</u>, Johnson was able to replicate this study. • This study has, <u>therefore</u>, been replicated many times. • <u>When</u> this study was replicated by Johnson (20xx), the results were identical. • <u>Specifically</u>, this study was replicated by Johnson in 20xx. • <u>For example</u>, Johnson (20xx) was able to replicate this study.
• <u>Because of</u> the unfavorable economic conditions...	• <u>Due to</u> the unfavorable economic conditions... • <u>This is because of</u> the unfavorable economic conditions. • <u>Since</u> the unfavorable economic conditions continue... • <u>As</u> the unfavorable economic conditions continue...

🔒 Exercise 6C-1: But, And, So & Because

次の 1 ~ 10 の文を読み、下線の部分を別紙を用いて直しなさい。文によっては下線の部分を直すのに文全体の構成を変える必要もあるので注意すること。

1. The number of non-Japanese living in Japan is increasing every year. <u>So</u> intercultural marriages have become much more common recently.
2. <u>But,</u> society's acceptance of those marriages seems to depend largely on the nationality and race of the non-Japanese individual.
3. <u>And</u> marrying a Caucasian seems to be much more acceptable than marrying another Asian. . .
4. <u>Because</u> culture and language are inextricably linked, to become truly proficient in a foreign language, one must also study the culture in which that language is being used.
5. <u>And,</u> the best way to learn about culture and language is to actually live in a country where the language is spoken.
6. <u>So</u> "homestaying" has become very popular among students.
7. <u>But</u> one must not assume that going abroad guarantees increased cultural sensitivity.
8. <u>Because,</u> research has revealed that contact with foreign cultures alone is not enough to foster cultural sensitivity.
9. <u>And,</u> contact with people from different cultures can result in reinforcing negative stereotypes of people of that culture.
10. <u>So,</u> it can be said that one must be very careful when preparing for and choosing a homestay program.

B

Word Choice

Inappropriate for Formal Writing	Possible Alternatives
"I think . . ." や "I feel . . ." 等の一人称単数代名詞はなるべくさける	"I think . . ." や "I feel . . ." 等を省くだけでもよいが、下記のような表現を使うこともできる。 "This is . . ." "According to Smith (20xx) . . ." "It can be argued . . ." "Many writers have argued . . ."
日本人の学生はよく "had better" を使うが、ネイティブスピーカーが聞くとまるで脅しのように聞こえてしまうので避けた方がよい。 *Americans had better understand the Japanese culture.	* It is important for Americans to understand the Japanese culture. * It is crucial for Americans to understand the Japanese culture.
"Japan has a peculiar culture." 日本人の学生はよく「特有な」という意味で "peculiar" を使うが、peculiar という言葉には「変な」、「妙な」などというマイナスな意味も含まれている。"Unique" という言葉にはプラスのイメージがあるので、その方が好ましい。	"Japan has a unique culture."

160

Exercise 6C-2: Word Choice

次の 1～8 の文を読み、下線の部分を別紙を用いて直しなさい。文によっては下線の部分を直すのに文全体の構成を変える必要があるので、文全体を書き直しなさい。

1. I feel that the world is becoming increasingly interdependent.

2. In this paper, I want to talk about cultural differences in the business setting.

3. Some researchers claim that the concept of "honne" and "tatemae" are peculiar to Japanese culture.

4. I think that businesses had better adjust their management practices as well as their products to the host country.

5. Of the three theories, I feel that Smith's (1973) is most commonly cited by other researchers.

6. I think that every culture is peculiar.

7. Students had better read a lot if they would like to be good writers.

8. I feel that the hardest part of writing a paper is to be persistent and resilient.

C

Grammar & Mechanics

　学生の論文を読んでいて一番気になるのがスペルミスである。なぜならば前述の通り、スペリングは、コンピューターを使えばすぐに直せるからである。特に "r" と "l" が逆になっているケースが目につくので注意して欲しい。スペリング以外にも、よく見かける細かいミスを幾つかここで紹介する。

一般論を述べている時に、性別を指定する言葉はなるべく避けるべきである。 * Before going abroad, it is important for a businessman to learn not only the language but the culture of the country he is going to.	これに関して統一した解決法はないようである。対処法は人それぞれである。He を使い続けている人もいれば全部 she にしている人もいる。人によっては章ごとに入れ替えている人もいる。アメリカとイギリスの違いもありそうだ。最近アメリカでよくみかけるのは he/she 等を避けるために下記のように複数形を使う方法である。 *Before going abroad, it is important for individuals/businesspeople to not only learn the language but the culture of the country they are going to.
単語が 2 行にわたるときは必ずシラブルの区切りに従って分け、ハイフンを各行の最後につけること。よく見受ける間違いはシラブルとは関係ないところで区切ったり、ハイフンを行末ではなく行頭に置くことである。[2]	○　be-tween 　　　　　　　　　×　betw-een 　　　　　　　　　×　be-tween

---

2　Microsoft Word 等を使う場合、何もしなくても自動的にコンピューターが処理してくれる。

子音で始まる語の前では"a"を用い、母音で始まる語の前では"an"を用いる。この場合の子音・母音の区別は、綴り字ではなく、発音による。 例えば"university"の場合は発音が [you-nih-ver-si-ty] なので "a university" が正しい。	× an university 　（発音：you-nih-ver-si-ty） ○ a university × an one-year stay abroad 　（発音：won） ○ a one-year stay abroad × a honest person 　（発音：o-nest） ○ an honest person
"It's" や "that's" 等の短縮形は会話等では自然であるが、論文では使わない。	"It is" や "that is" 等と短縮しないで書く。

Exercise 6C-3:　総合練習

次の 1 ～ 10 の文を読み、誤っている部分を見つけ、直しなさい。文によっては1つ以上誤っているところがあるので注意すること。

1. Before discussing what companies should do in the 21st century, I want to first talk about the situation in which companies today find themselves.

2. I think that selecting an university can be a difficurt decision.

3. Before going abroad, a businessman had better study the languagespoken in the country he is assigned to.

4. Many books on writing state that if a man wants to become a good writer, he had better read a lot.

5. But reading a lot can be very time consuming.

6. So it's important for you to be selective about what you read.

7. Because what you read will inevitably affect the way you write.

8. This doesn't mean that you should try to copy other people's writing styles.

9. Their styles are peculiar to them and shouldn't be imitated.

10. Because, I think that writing is a form of artistic expression.

論文を書く際、適切な表現を習得するために、下記の参考書類を熟読するとよい。
- 日向清人 (2013). 即戦力がつく英文ライティング. 東京：三省堂印刷.
- Strunk, W. Jr., & White, E. B. (1999). The Elements of Style (4th ed.). New York: MacMillan Publishing.

6D Formatting the Paper
形式を整える

　学術誌に論文を提出する場合や授業の課題などは厳密に要求されるスタイルに沿って書かなくてはいけないが、特に指定がない場合は次のガイドラインを参照するとよい。

- Microsoft Word などを利用している場合はTimes New Roman12ポイントが読みやすい
- 行間は1.5に設定して書くと書き直す時に十分スペースがある
- 各ページの右上にレポートの題名とページ数を書く（次ページを参照）
- 各paragraphの頭を5スペース分indent[3]する
- Period（.）の後は1スペース分開ける
- Margins（余白）は上下、左右、各2.5センチずつとる（下記を参照）

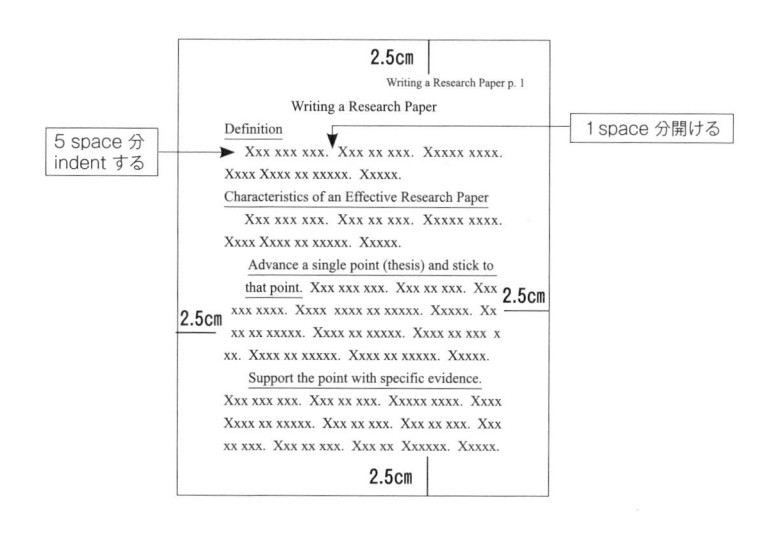

3　indent - 他の行より下げて（引っ込めて）書く

Title Page（表紙）

　Title Page は必ずしも必要ではないが、一般には下記のような Title Page を付けるとよいだろう（下の例は授業で提出するレポートの場合）。ただし、表紙や目次等は論文の枚数には含まれないので注意すること。

```
            レポートの題名　ページ数

              レポートの題名

                    by
                   名前


                 先生の名前
                  科目名
                   日付
```

→

```
                        Using Movies to Teach Culture p.1

               Using Movies to Teach
                      Culture

                        by
                    Taro Yamada


                  Tomoko Yoshida
                  English Composition
                    March 3, 2015
```

Title の書き方：

A good title should be like a good metaphor;[4] it should intrigue without being too baffling or too obvious.
　　　　　　　Walker Percy (cited in Charlton, 1997. p. 114)

- Title は論文のテーマを簡潔に表わす単語またはフレーズである。完結した sentence である必要はない。
- Percyが上記で述べている通り、論文や本のタイトルとは、本論の比喩のようなものである。読者の興味を引くために、少しミステリアスな感じを残すとよい。また、コロン（：）の前には題名を短くまとめ、コロンの後には副題としてもう少し詳しく論文の内容を説明する場合が多い。
- また、題名を書くときには4文字以上の言葉は全て単語の先頭文字を大文字にする。ただし、冠詞や前置詞等は文の最初やコロン（：）の直後でない

4　metaphor - 比喩

限り小文字のままでよい。[5] この大文字と小文字の分け方の形式をtitle caseと呼ぶ。

Exercise 6D: Titles

下記1の例に沿って次の2～5のtitleを「題名：副題名」というスタイルに変更し、title case（大文字、小文字に注意）にしなさい。

例1. A Bribe or a Gift: Ethics in Doing Business Internationally

2. gender discrimination an examination of glass ceilings in five Japanese companies

3. apologies in Japan as a gateway to understanding Japanese culture

4. should age be a criteria for when entering universties?

5. Germany as a case study of effective recycling

Headingの書き方：

　論文につける見出しや小見出しも、分野や学術誌、そして指導教員によっても異なるので、あらかじめ調べておく必要がある。小見出しをまったく使わない方法もあれば、なるべく細かく区切る方法もあるからである。特定の学術誌に掲載するつもりで論文を書いている場合、その学術誌に記載されている論文の構成や小見出しの使い方を参考にするとよい。

　Headingの表示の仕方の一例として、ここでAPAスタイルのformatを

5　ただし参考文献リストを APA スタイルで書く時は文献の題名は学術誌名・雑誌名等を除き sentence style（文の先頭文字のみを大文字にする）で書くことになっている。

簡単に説明しておく。APA Manual はかなり細かく指定しているので、詳しくは Publication Manual of the American Psychological Association を参照するとよい。

　Heading というのは幾つかのレベルで存在している。まずは章の題名である。次のレベルに各セクションの見出しがある。場合によっては各セクションをさらに区切り、もっと細かい見出しがふえる。見出しや小見出しを見た時にすぐにどのレベルかわかるためにもレベルごとに format を変えることになっている。APA では5段階のレベルを指定している。(Figure 6-2 を参照)。レベルの数に応じて下記のレベルの形式に従い、順に足していく。例えばレベルが3つある場合はレベル1, 2, 3のみを使う。レベルが4つある場合は1, 2, 3, 4を使う。

☆ **Figure 6.2: APA Levels of Heading**

Level 1	**Title Case で書き、太文字にし、中央に置く**
Level 2	**Title Case で書き、太文字にし、左に揃える。**
Level 3	**インデントし、文の先頭文字のみ大文字で書き、period をつける。太文字にする。次の sentence は改行せずにつなげて書く。**
Level 4	***インデントし、文の先頭文字のみ大文字で書き、period をつける。イタリック体の太文字にする。次の sentence は改行せずにつなげて書く。***
Level 5	*インデントし、文の先頭文字のみ大文字で書き、period をつける。イタリック体にする。次の sentence は改行せずにつなげて書く。*

〈American Psychiatric Association (2010) にもとづき、筆者が作成〉

　例えば Reading 1B (14〜19ページ) は3つのレベルに分かれている。まずは題名がレベル1、Definition、Characteristics of an Effective Research Paper と Conclusion がレベル2、そして Advance a single point (thesis) and stick to that point 等がレベル3である。

ただし、これはあくまでも厳密に APA スタイルを使う場合である。通常授業等で提出するレポートではレベルごとに揃っていれば、どのような format を使っても構わない。特に最新のワープロソフト等を使えば色々な飾り文字等を作ることができ、より分かりやすくレベルの区別ができる。

☆ Figure 6.3: Headings for Reading 1B

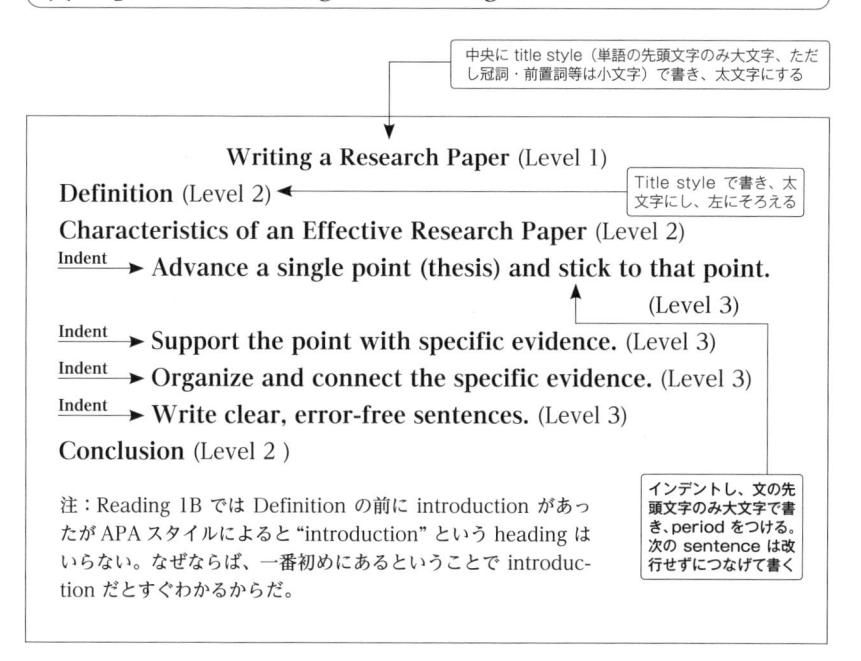

中央に title style（単語の先頭文字のみ大文字、ただし冠詞・前置詞等は小文字）で書き、太文字にする

Writing a Research Paper (Level 1)
Definition (Level 2) ← Title style で書き、太文字にし、左にそろえる
Characteristics of an Effective Research Paper (Level 2)
　Indent → **Advance a single point (thesis) and stick to that point.** (Level 3)
　Indent → **Support the point with specific evidence.** (Level 3)
　Indent → **Organize and connect the specific evidence.** (Level 3)
　Indent → **Write clear, error-free sentences.** (Level 3)
Conclusion (Level 2)

インデントし、文の先頭文字のみ大文字で書き、period をつける。次の sentence は改行せずにつなげて書く

注：Reading 1B では Definition の前に introduction があったが APA スタイルによると "introduction" という heading はいらない。なぜならば、一番初めにあるということで introduction だとすぐわかるからだ。

この本も3つのレベルに分かれているが、APA の format を使わずに自分で format を決めた。さらに、書きながら format を忘れないように Figure 6.4 のような一覧表を作った。これくらい書かなくても簡単に覚えられそうだが、実際に文章を書いていると太文字だったか白抜き文字だったか等と迷うものである。いちいち前の章に振り返って見るより、一覧表があったほうが、あとあと編集する時に楽である。

⭐ **Figure 6.4: Headings & Subheadings**

＊各章の title は大きな文字で書き、改行して、左に。

CHAPTER *1*　　(Level 1)

Overview：総論

＊各セクションの subheading は太文字で書き左に。

1A　Goals for This Book　　(Level 2)

＊Exercise 等は白抜き文字とし、colon（：）を付け、左に。

📖 **Reading 1A:**　　(Level 3)

✓ **Comprehension Check 1A:**　　(Level 3)

🔒 **Exercise 1B:**　　(Level 3)

✏ **Writing for Fun 1:**　　(Level 3)

🍎 **Applications 2B:**　　(Level 3)

📎 **Useful Expressions 2B:**　　(Level 3)

Table of Contents（目次）

　前述したように、論文を細かくセクションに分け、小見出しを付けたほうが、読みやすくなる。さらにわかりやすくするために目次を作り、どこに何があるかを表示するとよい。この本の目次を見てもわかるように、目次は基本的に見出しにページを明示したものである。

Using Movies to Teach Culture p.1

Table of Contents

Introduction　　p.2
Advantages　　p.3
Disadvantages　　p.4
Examples　　p.5
Conclusion　　p.6

Tables and Figures（表や図）

　研究結果等は表や図を使ったほうがわかりやすい場合が多い。表や図を挿入する場合は、本文にも表や図の解釈や説明を入れる必要がある。本文で説明する時によりわかりやすいように Table 1、Figure 1 等と表示しておくとよい。何章もある本や論文の場合は「Table 1.2: Consumption Trends」（第1章の2番目の消費傾向に関する表）等と表示するとよい。なお、表や図の使い過ぎは逆に論文を読みにくくするため、全体で5～6個以内に留めるように。

Appendix（付録）

　研究等で使ったアンケートのサンプル等長いものを入れる場合は、論文の最後に Appendix（付録）として入れるとよい。その場合も Appendix A、Appendix B 等と表示し、title をつけるとよい。

> Appendix A: Sample Questionnaire
> Xx xx xx x x. Xx xx x xx x . Xx xxx xxx xxx xxx. Xxx xx x xxx xxx x xxx.
> 1. Xxxxxx xxx x xxx xx? _____
> 2. Xxxxxx xxx x xxx xx? _____
> 3. Xxxxxx xxx x xxx xx? _____
> 4. Xxxxxx xxx x xxx xx? _____
> 5. Xxxxxx xxx x xxx xx? _____

References

　ここでは論文の中で引用した文献を全て著者の苗字を基準にアルファベット順に記すこと。論文のために読んだ文献でも引用しなかったものは書かなくてよい。References の書き方は第4章で述べた通り、分野によって異なるが、ここでは APA スタイル（97～101ページ参照）の例を挙げる。

References

Kaplan, R. B. (1966). Cultural thought patterns in intercultural education. *Language Learning: A Journal of Applied Linguistics, 16* (1 & 2), 1–20.

Langan, J. (1985). *College writing skills with readings.* New York, NY: McGraw-Hill Book Company.

Okabe, R. (1993). 日本のレトリック [Japan's rhetoric]. In M. Hashimoto & S. Ishii (Eds.). 日本人のコミュニケーション [*Japanese communication styles*] (pp. 55–81). Tokyo: Kirihara-shoten.

Oshima, A., & Hogue, A. (1978). *Writing academic English* (2nd ed.). Menlo Park, CA: Addisson-Wesley Publishing Company.

Roberts, W. H. (1985). *The writer's companion: A short handbook.* Boston, MA: Little, Brown and Company.

Writing for Fun 6: TOEFL Writing その2

TOEFL Writing の練習は回数をこなすのが重要であるため、また挑戦してみよう。できれば、毎日一つの課題を選び、挑戦するとよい。トピックの例は Google で "TOEFL Writing Topics" と検索すれば出てくる。

Do you agree or disagree with the following statement? Watching television is bad for children. Use specific details and examples to support your answer.

References

American Psychiatric Association (2010). *Publication manual of the American Psychological Association* (6th edition). Washington, DC: Author.

Bryant, D. (1992). Writing is rewriting. In T. Clark, W. Brohaugh, B. Woods & B. Strickland (Eds.), *The writer's digest handbook of novel writing* (pp. 182-189). Cincinnati, OH: Writer's Digest Books.

Charlton, J. (Ed.). 1997. *The writer's quotation book: A literary companion.* Winchester, MA: Faber & Faber.

Gardner, J. (1983). *On becoming a novelist.* New York, NY: Harper & Row.

Obstfeld, R. (1992). Finish that novel before it finishes you. In T. Clark, W. Brohaugh, B. Woods & B. Strickland (Eds.), *The writer's digest handbook of novel writing* (pp. 190-195). Cincinnati, OH: Writer's Digest Books.

解答例

Comprehension Check の解答は、なるべく自然な英語になれてもらうため、Reading のなかとは異なる表現を使ったり、省略した形をとったりしている。

★Comprehension Check 1A:

1. The skills needed to write a good research paper.   2. Part I.   3. Chapters 2-4.   4. Chapter 4.   5. The three main components of an academic report and advice on how to finish a paper.   6. a. A better understanding of what good academic writing is.   6. b. The actual experience of writing a research paper.

★Comprehension Check 1B:

1. No.   2. To understand the definition, components and purposes of an English research paper.   3. To present an original thesis and prove it.   4. To advance a single point (thesis) and stick to that point, to support the point with specific evidence, to organize and connect the specific evidence, and to write clear, error-free sentences.   5. What is "logical" in one culture may not be in another.   6. Going through the published literature to locate relevant material.   7. Is it relevant? Is it reliable?   8. Chronological order, logical division, cause & effect, and comparison & contrast.   9. Chronological order, logical division.   10. Since most word processing programs have a spell-check mechanism.

174

★Writing for Fun 1:

#1

> 1-1-1 Hiyoshi
> Kohoku-ku, Yokohama-shi
> Kanagawa-ken Japan 211-0003
>
> January 4, 2015
>
> Mr. Paul Parker
> Director of Human Resources
> Parker Company
> 51 Duke Street
> Cambridge MA 00000, USA
>
> Dear Mr. Paul Parker:
>
> I recently learned about a possible part-time job at your company. I am currently a second year student at XX University and am majoring in Business & Commerce. I have been very interested in your company since I was a child. I was, therefore, very excited to hear that your company had an opening for a part-time position. It would be a true honor to be able to apply for this position.
>
> Could you kindly send an application packet as well as other relevant information to the following address?
>
> > Hanako Keio
> > 1-1-1 Hiyoshi, Kohoku-ku
> > Yokohama-shi 211-0003 Japan
>
> Thank you very much in advance for your cooperation! I look forward to hearing from you soon!
>
> Sincerely yours,
> *Hanako Keio*
> Hanako Keio

#2

1-1-1 Hiyoshi
Kohoku-ku, Yokohama-shi
Kanagawa-ken Japan 211-0003

January 4, 2015

Ms. Pauline Abe
Admissions Office
ABC University
1287 Prospect Street
Honolulu, Hawaii 96815
USA

Dear Ms. Pauline Abe:

I recently learned about your summer intensive English program through a professor at my university. I am currently a first year student at XX University and am hoping to study at ABC University next year as an exchange student. For this reason, I am very interested in enrolling in your summer intensive English program so that I might be better prepared to handle your rigorous curriculum next year.

Could you kindly send an application packet as well as other relevant information to the following address?

    Hanako Keio
    1-1-1 Hiyoshi, Kohoku-ku
    Yokohama-shi 211-0003 Japan

Thank you very much in advance for your cooperation! I look forward to hearing from you soon!

Sincerely yours,

Hanako Keio
Hanako Keio

★Comprehension Check 2A:

1. It is likely to be shallow and uninteresting.
2. Is this topic specific enough for me to cover within the given amount of space? What aspect of this topic interests me the most? What aspect of this topic am I knowledgeable about?

★Exercise 2A-1:

（決まった解答はない。）

★Exercise 2A-2:

1. Japanese and American (group) Communication Styles: A Comparative Analysis (S&D)
2. Three (number) Effective Ways (aspect) to Help Save the Environment (C&E)
3. A Comparison of Universities (S&D) in Three (number) Cultures: Japan, Germany & the USA (place)
4. Is Racism an Issue in Japan (place)?
5. Examining the Glass Ceiling (aspect) in Five (number) Japanese Companies (place)
6. Business Etiquette (aspect) in Korea (place)

★Comprehension Check 2B:

1. Reports, speeches, product development and campaign slogans. 2. It is a technique in which individuals allow themselves to think of as many different ideas as possible without passing judgment on them. 3. Ideas are not discarded or laughed at because they seem strange or out of place. 4. They interfere with the train of thought. 5. It is not random, it is organized.

★Exercises 2B-1, 2B-2, 2B-3 & 2B-4:

（決まった解答はない。）

★Exercise 2C-1:

1. c   2. e   3. d   4. b   5. a

★Exercise 2C-2:

（決まった解答はない。）

★Writing for Fun 2:

Situation 1:

To: purdy@purdy.com
cc: jones@jones.com ← 会議の議事録は上司にも見てもらった方がいいのでcc: する。
Subject: Minutes from our last meeting

Dear Mr. Paul Purdy,
cc: Janet Jones ← Jonesさんをcc: していることを明らかにするために、ここにも記入する。

Thank you so much for making time out of your busy schedule to meet with us yesterday. As promised, I am attaching a copy of the minutes from our meeting. I would appreciate it if you could please take a look at it to make sure that everything is accurate.

Thank you once again and we look forward to seeing you again soon!

Sincerely,
Hanako Keio

****

Hanako Keio
Assistant Director, Marketing Department
Keio Motors, 4-1-1 Hiyoshi
Kohoku-ku, Yokohama-shi, Kanagawa-ken 223-8521
Tel:###-###-####
Fax: ###-###-###
Email: hanakokeio@example.com
Web site: http://hanako-keio.example-com

議事録を添付し忘れないように！

Situation 2:

To: svenson@svenson.com
cc: yoshida@yoshidauniversity.ac.jp
Subject: Possible position at your company

> 吉田先生の紹介なので必ずcc:する。本当に吉田先生の紹介であるという証明にもなるうえ、cc:しておくことによって吉田先生がフォローしてくれるかもしれない。

Dear Ms. Svenson,
cc: Dr. Yoshida

My name is Hanako Keio and I am a second year student at XX University. My professor, Dr. Tomoko Yoshida, mentioned that you have a part-time position available in your marketing department. I am currently studying business and commerce and my dream is to work in a marketing department in the future. For this reason, it would be beneficial for me to gain some practical experience along with my academic education. I would be very honored if you could consider me for this position. Please find attached my CV and a recommendation letter from Dr. Yoshida.

I look forward to hearing from you soon.

Sincerely,
Hanako Keio

****
Hanako Keio
Assistant Director, Marketing Department
Keio Motors, 4-1-1 Hiyoshi
Kohoku-ku, Yokohama-shi, Kanagawa-ken 223-8521
Tel:###-###-####
Fax: ###-###-###
Email: hanakokeio@example.com
Web site: http://hanako-keio.example-com

> 履歴書と教員の推薦書を添付するように。

★Exercise 3A-1:

（ここであげた解答はあくまでも例であって同じである必要はない。）
1. sequential, logical   2. comparison & contrast   3. chronological
4. cause & effect   5. comparison & contrast   6. cause & effect
7. logical, cause & effect   8. chronological, logical   9. chronological
10. logical, sequential

★Exercise 3A-2:

（決まった解答はない。）

★Comprehension Check 3B:

1. c)   2. The writer can get a general idea of what the final paper will be like and make alterations if necessary.   3. No.   4. Is the main point clear? Are the supporting arguments, data or examples convincing? Can everything be covered within the available amount of space? Is there anything that should be included or omitted?

★Exercise 3B-1:

（ここであげた解答はあくまでも例であって同じである必要はない。）
Reading 2B
I. Introduction—Main idea: Once you have chosen and narrowed down your topic, you can start brainstorming.
II. How to brainstorm:
　A. Write the topic at the top of the paper.
　B. Think about the topic and jot down as many words or phrases you can think of.
　　1. Brainstorm in Japanese or English.
　　2. Don't try to make complete sentences; don't worry about spelling or grammar.
　　3. Don't evaluate if it is good or not.
　　4. Write everything in random order.
　　5. Do it in a quiet place.
　　6. Carry the brainstorming sheet with you.
III. Another method of brainstorming is mindmapping.

IV. Organizing your brainstorming sheet.
V. Conclusion—As a result of brainstorming or mindmapping, you should now have a rough idea of what you will be writing about.

Reading 3B
I. Introduction—Main Idea: Many writers find outlining an essential tool to writing well.
II. How to make an outline based on your brainstorming sheet.
III. Questions to ask yourself once the outline is made.
IV. Conclusion—The main advantage to making an outline is that one can examine the paper as a whole to see whether the arguments are clear and logical before actually writing it.

★Exercise 3B-2:

（決まった解答はない。）

★Writing for Fun 3:

（決まった解答はない。）

★Comprehension Check 4A:

1. Get sufficient background information on a topic. Give evidence to support your thesis.　　2. Use the library catalog, computer database, reference lists found at the end of articles and books.　　3. Yes.　4. 国立国会図書館サーチ.　　5. The library database such as EBSCO Host or CiNii.　　6. They are more up-to-date.　　7. Yes—to access a wide variety of materials; to gain an edge over others when publishing.　8. Label and file them.

★Comprehension Check 4B:

1. Plagiarism.　　2. Yes.　　3. The page number.　　4. It makes writing seem fragmented.　　5. No.　　6. Paraphrasing and summarizing.　　7. No.　8. Advantages include being able to copy and paste notes directly into the paper afterwards. Disadvantages include lack of accuracy.
 9. Taking notes directly on the article; inputting information directly into the computer.

★Exercise 4B-1:
（解答省略）

★Exercise 4B-1:
（ここであげた解答はあくまでも例であって同じである必要はない。）

1. Paraphrase: According to Sobel and Klein (1996), exercise is much better for your back than any type of medication. They claim that it is the preferred choice not only because it is effective but because it has no side effects and is inexpensive. This stands in sharp contrast to painkillers and anti-inflammatory medications that are usually prescribed for people with back pain. Although these drugs are the most common treatment for back pain, the research has revealed that they are not only ineffective but also have unpleasant side effects that may cause considerable harm.
   Summary: According to Sobel and Klein (1996), exercise is much better for back pain than any type of medication. Their research has revealed that although most doctors prescribe painkillers and anti-inflammatory medications to patients with back pains, those medications are not only ineffective but can have unpleasant side effects that may cause considerable harm.

2. Paraphrase: An early study conducted in France has shown that drinking a moderate amount of wine daily can help prevent Alzheimer's disease. The reasons, however, are still unclear "Health report," 1997, April, p. 14).
   Summary: Initial findings have revealed that drinking a moderate amount of wine daily can help prevent Alzheimer's disease ("Health report" 1997, April, p. 14).

3. Paraphrase: Research has revealed that people who socialize a lot are less likely to catch a cold. Even though they are probably exposed to more germs, the psychological effects of socializing seem to help keep the immune system strong ("Health report," 1997, July , p. 14).
   Summary: Research has shown that people who socialize a lot are less likely to catch a cold "Health report," 1997, July , p. 14).

4. Paraphrase: Pregnant women should avoid exposure to cigarette

smoke. Research has revealed that even small amounts of passive smoke can significantly increase the odds of giving birth to a baby with lung problems. The smoke blocks the oxygen flow from the mother to the fetus and thus causes damage while the baby is still in the mother's uterus ("Health report," 1997, April, p. 16).

Summary: Research has revealed that even small amounts of passive smoke to pregnant women can significantly increase the odds of giving birth to a baby with lung problems ("Health report," 1997, April, p. 16).

5. Paraphrase: The amount of time spent sitting is more important than the type of chair you sit on. Since sitting is worse for your back than standing or lying down, try to limit your sitting time as much as possible. When sitting down for long periods of time, try to take frequent breaks to stand up and stretch. Although this is easier to do at home, try to do the same at work too. When driving on long car trips take frequent breaks to stretch out. On long plane flights, try to stand and walk around the aisles whenever possible (Sobel & Klein, 1996).

Summary: Sobel and Klein (1996) claim that the amount of time spent sitting is more important the type of chair people sit on. Their advice is to stand up and stretch frequently whenever possible.

★Exercise 4C-1:

1. Hogue   2. 2006   3. Palgrave Macmillan   4. UK   5. Editors
6. Book chapter   7. The construction and validation of a measure of ethno-cultural identity conflict   8. Journal of Personality Assessment
9. 7 things the most interesting people all have in common   10. The Japan Times

★Exercise 4C-2:

1. Yashiro, K., Machi, E., Koike, H., & Yoshida, T. (2009). 異文化トレーニング：ボーダレス社会を生きる[Intercultural training: Living in a borderless society]. Tokyo: Sanshusha.
2. Condon, J. C., & Masumoto, T.(2011). *With respect to the Japanese : A guide for Americans.* Yarmouth, ME:Intercultural Press.
3. Shaules, J. (2007). The debate about cultural difference: Deep cul-

ture, cultural identity, and culture's influence on behavior. *Journal of Intercultural Communication*, 10, 115-132
4. Suzuki, Y. (2010, June). 部下が悪いのか？―多様化する職場の中でのコミュニケーション[Is it the subordinate's fault?: Communication in an increasingly multicultural work environment]．人事院月報 [National Personnel Authority Monthly Reports], 36-39.
5. White, M. (1988). *The Japanese overseas: Can they go home again?* London: The Free Press.
6. Ebuchi, K. (1986). 異文化適応のメカニズム ― 文化人類学的考察 [The mechanism of cultural adaptation: An anthropological study]. 教育と医学 *[Education and Medicine]*, 10, 910-948.
7. Brabant, M., Watson, B., & Gallois, C. (2007). Psychological perspectives: Social psychology, language, and intercultural communication. In H. Kotthoff, & H. Spencer-Oatey (Eds.), *Handbook of intercultural communication* (pp. 55-76). Berlin, Germany: Mouton de Gruyter.
8. Komisarof, A. (2010). Conflicting acculturation strategies regarding ethnocultural diversity: Towards a resolution for Japan's multicultural future. 異文化コミュニケーション[*Journal of Intercultural Communication*], 13, 31-38.
9. Muro, M. (2001). 異文化ミスコミュニケーション[Intercultural Miscommunication]. Tokyo: Seibido.

★Exercise 4C-3:（2014年11月現在）

2.	東京本館書庫*	請求記号：GB63-B273	＊複数ある場合はこちらには、一ヵ所だけ明記してある
3.	東京新館書庫	請求記号：Z6-B956	
4.	東京新館書庫	請求記号：Z2-57	
5.	東京本館書庫	請求記号：EC225-A32	
6.	デジタルデータ	請求記号：Z7-193	
7.	東京本館書庫	請求記号：KE23-B16	
8.	東京新館書庫	請求記号：Z6-B956	
9.	東京本館書庫	請求記号：Y45-H248	

★Writing for Fun 4:

(解答省略)

★Exercise 5A-1:

1. (ii), (i), (iii), (iv)   2. (i), (ii), (iii), (iv)   3. (i), (ii), (iii), (iv)

★Exercise 5A-2:

1. a   2. c   3. b

★Exercise 5A-3:

1. e   2. d   3. a   4. c   5. b
（分析の例は省略）

★Exercise 5A-4:

（ここであげた解答はあくまでも例であって同じである必要はない。）

1. Although the issue of government officials receiving bribes from businesses has been acknowledged as a serious problem in Japan for many years, it is still a common occurrence (Einhorn & Reynolds, 2014).
2. A visit to a freezing cold office building during the hot summer can be a shocking experience for the environmentally conscious person.
3. Although being a "mother" is a full-time job with no vacations, strangely enough, it does not come with the benefits normally associated with a full-time job such as a salary, paid vacations and health insurance.
4. Although Japan still claims to be a homogeneous society, the number of non-Japanese living in Japan has significantly increased during the past 20 years. In fact, according to the Japan Statistical Yearbook (2015), the number of registered non-Japanese living in Japan increased from 1,075,317 in 1990 to 2,066,455 in 2013.
5. Most Japanese spend their childhood preparing for university entrance examinations, which supposedly hold the key to their success or failure in life (Lewis, 2015).

★Exercise 5A-5:

（ここであげた解答はあくまでも例であって同じである必要はない。）

a. In fact, it is well documented that many individuals learn most about their own culture by going abroad and living in another county

(Shaules, 2007).
b. For a number of years now, the role of sexual differentiation in the process of childhood socialization has been of interest and concern to psychologists and feminists (e.g., Friedman & Downey, 2014; Witt, 1997).
c. N/A
d. Although the importance of reducing the amount of packaging is widely recognized, manufacturers continue to use an excessive amount of packaging for their products.
e. N/A

★Exercise 5A-6:
（ここであげた解答はあくまでも例であって同じである必要はない。）
2. I. Introduction - Thesis: If we are to help returnees take advantage of their unique experiences abroad, we need to help them resolve these issues. For returnees to become truly comfortable with their identity as a multicultural individual, however, society needs to change as well.
   II. Description of identity issues experienced by returnees
   III. A model returnees can use to help overcome the identity issues they are facing
   IV. A discussion of society's role
   V. Concrete suggestions
   VI. Conclusion
3. I. Introduction - Thesis: For effective learning to occur, lectures and reading assignments need to be followed up with assignments that require students to use the knowledge and skills acquired.
   II. Recent research supporting the importance of having students actively participate in the learning process
   III. The ratio of "hearing" to "seeing," and "doing" in an average university course
   IV. Specific ways in which "doing" can be incorporated into the classroom setting
   V. Conclusion

★Exercise 5A-7:

（ここであげた解答はあくまでも例であって同じである必要はない。）

2. This paper first provides a description of identity issues experienced by returnees. It will then proceed by presenting a model returnees can use to help overcome their identity issues and conclude by discussing society's role while offering concrete suggestions.
3. This paper first provides a summary of recent research supporting the importance of having students actively participate in the learning process. Next, it will present the ratio of "hearing" to "seeing," and "doing" in an average university course. Specifically, this chapter discusses ways in which "doing" can be incorporated into the classroom setting.

★Exercise 5B-1:

1. e   2. c   3. d   4. a   5. b

★Exercise 5B-2:

（ここであげた解答はあくまでも例であって同じである必要はない。）

a. In sum, what is considered a "perfectly appropriate gift" can differ across cultures.
b. Since Japan is such a small tight-knit society, human relationships play a large role in one's personal as well as professional life. Apologies thus serve the important role of ensuring smooth relationships with others.
c. Although, on the surface, Japanese companies have instituted Equal Employment Opportunity, many invisible barriers still exist to prevent women from being hired or promoted to executive level positions.

★Exercise 5B-3:

2. In sum, it can be said that identity is a serious issue that needs to be addressed by most returnees. Many returnees, years after their initial return to Japan, still claim to be struggling with their identity. Clearly, identity issues cannot be resolved overnight. This study has, howev-

er, revealed that identity models such as the ones introduced here can significantly reduce the amount of reverse culture shock experienced by returnees. Unfortunately, few schools with special quotas for returnees provide special training or classes to help returnees deal with the issue of identity. If schools with special quotas for returnees are indeed interested in fostering the returnees' uniqueness, identity issues need to be addressed in a systematic manner.

3. The amount of "doing" in the present university education system is very limited. As mentioned earlier, however, it would be far too time-consuming for students to actually experience everything firsthand. Thus, listening to lectures and reading books add efficiency while expanding the possibility of what students can learn. Passive forms of learning such as listening and reading, however, are easily forgotten. Thus, it is recommended that lectures and reading materials be supplemented by fieldwork exercises that enable students to apply what they have learned.

★Exercise 5C-1:

（解答省略）

★Exercise 5C-2:

1. C,E,A,B,D,
2. D,C,B,E,A 又は A,D,C,B,E
3. C,B,A,D
4. C,B,D,A,E

★Writing for Fun 5:

Whether to hire an inexperienced worker at a lower salary or an experienced worker at a higher salary depends on many variables such as whether the prospective employees are likely to stay in my company for the remainder of their careers, the types of positions I need to fill, and my immediate needs. I would carefully consider these three variables while weighing in the advantages and disadvantages of each option. ← (iii) Thesis statement

This essay will first discuss the three variables I must consider and then the advantages and disadvantages of each option.

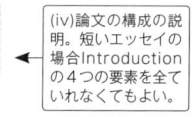

With regard to the first condition, the situation may vary depending on where my company is located. For example, if I were in the United States, where individuals normally move from one job to another, then I would assume that the individuals I am hiring will not stay with my company for the rest of their careers. In that case, I am more likely to hire individuals with enough skills to fulfill their duties immediately. If I were in Japan, although things are changing, individuals are more likely to stay much longer. In that case, I might be more likely to hire younger candidates and invest time and money on training them.

In terms of the second condition, if it was an upper management position, then clearly I would most likely need an experienced worker at a higher salary while a middle management position might be filled by a less experienced candidate. The third condition comes into play as well. If I am amply staffed then, it would be possible to hire inexperienced candidates and spend time training them while if our company needs staff to immediately take charge and produce results, then we will need more experienced candidates.

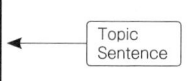

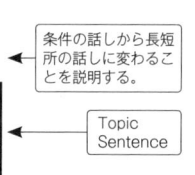

Let us now move on to the advantages and disadvantages of hiring the two types of workers. One of the advantages to hiring younger, inexperienced individuals is that it will be easier to train them to suit my needs and preferences. At the same time, their salaries will be much lower. The disadvantages include money and time spent on training, the possibility that they might move to another company after they are trained, and that they might not be able to contribute to the company immediately.

One of the most obvious advantages to hiring older, experienced personnel is that they will be able to do their job immediately. Additionally, they can bring in new ideas and know-how gained from their previous experiences. At the same time, their previous experiences can prevent them from learning my company's way of working. Their salaries will also be higher.

← Topic Sentence

With the above mentioned advantages and disadvantages in mind, I would consider the three variables mentioned at the beginning of the essay and determine which candidate will be the best choice.

← まとめ

Exercise 6B-1:

1. In the 1970s, when Japanese companies first started sending large numbers of employees abroad, returnee "problems" surfaced (Japan Overseas Educational Services, 1991). Children who grew up outside of Japan would return only to find that they could not adapt to schools in Japan and could not get into high schools or universities (Japan Overseas Educational Services, 1991).
2. Throughout history, there have been various methods of studying culture. Psychologists typically take a micro-approach to cultural study, while sociologists analyze culture through more of a macro lens.
3. School Inspections are an important part of education in England. One of the researchers, who observed part of a three-day workshop designed for school managers given over the course of several weeks, found the following about school inspections.
4. Returnees differ in their overseas experience in terms of the country or countries they lived in, the type of schools they attended, the number of years they spent abroad and their exposure to local culture.

Despite this variation, some generalizations have been made regarding interpersonal problems most commonly experienced by returnees.
5. Over the course of their educational tenure, students are presented with a myriad of approaches that seek to improve their overall educational experience. The traditional teacher–student relationship has been supplemented with new modes of education that aim to create opportunities for improved student outcomes (e.g., Lewis et al., 2007; Shameem & Tickoo, 1999; Short, 1999).
6. Fantini (1995) points out that too often language teachers neglect teaching culture while interculturalists downplay the importance of language. He also argues that language and culture go hand in hand, each influencing the other.
7. Often students at large universities feel at a loss and lack a sense of belonging. Learning Communities create a medium through which they can engage in social interaction with individuals who have similar goals and can work cooperatively with them to attain those goals.
8. Not only is social interaction an effective way to learn language, culture, and attain a new worldview, but it is also a powerful way to motivate students. Many studies in the field of Higher Education (e.g., Astin, 1984; Pascarella & Terenzini, 1980, 1991; Tinto, 1975, 1993, 1997) have revealed the importance of student involvement and integration in retaining students in colleges and universities.
9. Although Japan remained fairly closed to foreigners for many years, recently there has been an influx in the number of foreign permanent residents. Compared to 1975 when there were only 751,842 registered foreigners in Japan, by 2010, the number almost tripled to 2,134,151 (法務省, 2010). With this increase has been an increase in international marriages (厚生労働省, 2004) and children who are biethnic.
10. With the world becoming more global, many individuals are finding themselves growing up in the interstices of cultures. Some are born in their passport countries and later move to another country while others are born and raised outside of their passport countries (Schaetti, 1999). Some maintain their original nationality while others do not.

★Exercise 6B-2:
1. "They can because they think they can." —Virgil
2. "Every artist was first an amateur." — Ralph Waldo Emerson
3. "Education is the most powerful weapon which you can use to change the world." Nelson Mandela
4. "Every student can learn, just not on the same day, or the same way." — George Evans
5. "Live as if you were to die tomorrow. Learn as if you were to live forever."— Mahatma Gandhi
6. "Tell me and I forget, teach me and I may remember, involve me and I learn." — Benjamin Franklin
7. "Do not forget small kindnesses and do not remember small faults." — Chinese Proverb
8. "To climb steep hills requires a slow pace at first."—William Shakespeare
9. "Try not to become a man of success but a man of value." — Albert Einstein
10. "A wise man will make more opportunities than he finds." — Francis Bacon

★Exercise 6C-1:
（ここであげた解答はあくまでも例であって同じである必要はない。157～158ページの表も例の一部である。したがって、表になくても解答にあげているものもある。）
1. For this reason, や As a result,　2. Unfortunately, や However,
3. Furthermore, や And を除いて Marrying で始める　4. Since や As
5. And, を除いて The で始める
6. As a result や This is why や For this reason　7. However,
8. Because, を除いて Research で始めるか、This is because ...
9. Furthermore, や In Fact,　10. Therefore,

★Exercise 6C-2:
（ここであげた解答はあくまでも例であって同じである必要はない。）
1. The world is becoming increasingly interdependent.
2. This paper will examine cultural differences in the business setting.

3. Some researchers claim that the concept of "honne" and "tatemae" are unique to Japanese culture.
4. It is important for businesses to adjust their management practices as well as their products to the host country.
5. Of the three theories, Smith's (1973) is most commonly cited by other researchers.
6. Every culture is unique.
7. It is important for students to read a lot if they would like to be good writers.
8. The hardest part of writing a paper is to be persistent and resilient.

★Exercise 6C-3:

（ここであげた解答はあくまでも例であって同じである必要はない。）

1. Before discussing what companies should do in the 21st century, this paper will first examine the situation in which companies today find themselves.
2. Selecting a university can be a difficult decision. （シラブルが一つしかない場合は割らない。）
3. Before going abroad, it is important for business people to study the language spoken in the country they are assigned to.
4. Many books on writing state that if individuals want to become good writers, it is important/essential for them to read a lot.
5. Unfortunately, reading a lot can be very time consuming.
6. It is, therefore, important for you to be selective about what you read.
7. This is because what you read will inevitably affect the way you write.
8. This does not mean that you should try to copy other people's writing styles.
9. Their styles are unique to them and should not be imitated.
10. This is because writing is a form of artistic expression.

★Exercise 6D : Titles

（ここであげた解答はあくまでも例であって同じである必要はない。）
1. なし
2. Gender Discrimination : An Examination of Glass Ceilings in Five Japanese Companies

3. Apologies in Japan: A Gateway to Understanding Japanese Culture
4. Criteria for Entering Universities: Does Age Matter?
5. Effective Recycling: Germany as a Case Study

★Writing for Fun 6:

Although at first glance, one might be inclined to agree that television is bad for children, reality is not that simple. This essay will discuss both positive as well as negative effects of television on children. ← Thesis / 論文の構成の説明

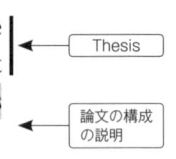

On the positive side, there are many educational TV programs available for children. Educational TV programs cover a wide span of topics from natural science to anthropology, history, sociology, and business. Television makes it possible for most children, not just the extremely rich, to see various animal, plant, and human life around the world. They can also learn from the foremost experts around the world, not simply from teachers at their schools. ← Topic Sentence

TV also provides news programs that inform us of current events. Unlike newspapers, TV news provides audio-visual footage to help better appreciate what happened. Another benefit of watching news on TV is that children can learn how difficult words are pronounced—if children only read, they sometimes know the meaning of a word but not how it is pronounced. ← Topic Sentence

Finally, even TV sitcoms and dramas can be educational. Children can watch the way people interact with each other, learn current language, social skills, and different value systems. Instead of simply assuming that all families are like their own families, they are given a chance to watch how other families and friends might interact. ← Topic Sentence

Of course, excessive TV viewing can cause many problems. If a child watches TV all day and does nothing else, the child might experience eye strain, headaches, and suffer from lack of exercise. If they snack while watching TV, obesity could also be a problem. Further, if they only watch TV and do not interact with peers their age, they would lose many important learning opportunities that can only be gained firsthand from interacting with friends and family. Another problem with TV is that because its purpose is to entertain, many of its shows are based on exaggeration, stereotypes, and inappropriate behavior. Excessive violence and sex are also prevalent. Children watching TV shows not suited for their age can be traumatized by what they see or can acquire a distorted view of reality. ← Topic Sentence

In sum, there is no simple answer to the question whether TV is good or bad for children. TV, like many things in life, can be both good and bad. If parents carefully monitor the amount of time spent and the types of shows their children watch, TV can be an extremely educational tool that teaches them many things. Unsupervised, it can lead to disastrous results. As in most things in life, the key is moderation and supervision. ← Conclusion

■ 著者紹介

吉田友子
Tomoko Yoshida

略　歴：1967年生まれ。シラキュース大学大学院修士号取得。ハワイ大学大学院博士号取得。現在, 慶應義塾大学商学部教授。
専　攻：異文化コミュニケーション
主な著書：*Improving Intercultural Interactions* (Richard Brislinと共著, Sage Publications, 1994), *Intercultural Communication Training: An Introduction* (Richard Brislinと共著, Sage Publications, 1994), Oded Shenkar (1995編) の *Global Perspectives of Human Resource Management* 内の Intercultural Skills and Recommended Behaviors: The Psychological Perspective for Training Programs を Dr. Richard Brislinと共著 (Prentice Hall), 異文化トレーニング (八代京子他と共著, 三修社 1998), Peers' Perceptions of Japanese Returnees (松本他と共著, *International Journal of Intercultural Relations*, 27, pp. 429-445, 2003), A longitudinal study of parent involvement as social capital in promoting college enrollment for diverse groups (博士論文, ハワイ大学), An Identity Based on Being Different: A Focus on Biethnic Individuals in Japan (及川と共著, *International Journal of Intercultural Relations*, 31, pp. 633-653, 2007), Different reactions to growing up biethnic in Japan (及川と共著, *Journal of Intercultural Communication*, 15, pp. 15-32, 2012), Intercultural Communication Skills: What Japanese Businesses Today Need (鈴木, 八代と共著, *International Journal of Intercultural Relations*, 37, pp. 72-85, 2013)。

アカデミックライティング入門　第2版
── 英語論文作成法 ──

1998年11月5日　初　版第1刷発行
2015年4月20日　第2版第1刷発行

著　者─────吉田友子
発行者─────坂上　弘
発行所─────慶應義塾大学出版会株式会社
　　　　　　　〒108-8346　東京都港区三田2-19-30
　　　　　　　TEL〔編集部〕03-3451-0931
　　　　　　　　　〔営業部〕03-3451-3584〈ご注文〉
　　　　　　　　　〔　〃　〕03-3451-6926
　　　　　　　FAX〔営業部〕03-3451-3122
　　　　　　　振替　00190-8-155497
　　　　　　　http://www.keio-up.co.jp/

本文組版・装丁──辻　聡
印刷・製本────中央精版印刷株式会社
カバー印刷────株式会社太平印刷社

©2015 Tomoko Yoshida
Printed in Japan　ISBN 978-4-7664-2212-2

慶應義塾大学出版会

英語論文の書き方入門

迫桂・徳永聡子著　学問の心得や英語論文ならではの特徴、テーマ探しから執筆・完成に至るまでの手順を、準備編と実践編にわけて詳しく解説する。はじめて英語論文に取り組む人にも、きちんと学び直したい人にも、よくわかる一冊。　◎2,000円

アカデミックライティング応用編
―文学・文化研究の英語論文作成法

アンドルー・アーマー、河内恵子、松田隆美、ウィリアム・スネル著　テーマの見つけ方、論文のフォーマット、分析的論述の方法など具体例を挙げて解説し、練習問題も交えて習熟できる良書。論文作成のためのワープロソフトの活用法も詳述する。大学生から大学院生以上対象。　◎2,000円

シカゴ・スタイル
研究論文執筆マニュアル

ケイト・L・トゥラビアン著／沼口隆・沼口好雄訳　初版刊行以来70年以上にわたって読み継がれている、学術論文の標準スタイルの一つである「シカゴ・マニュアル」に準拠した研究手法と論文執筆のためのガイドブック、その最新版を邦訳。　◎8,000円

表示価格は刊行時の本体価格（税別）です。

慶應義塾大学出版会

レポート・論文の書き方入門 第3版

河野哲也著　ロング＆ベストセラーの、初学者向けレポートの書き方決定版。画期的な練習方法の紹介をはじめ注や引用の豊富な実例が好評。第 3 版では情報倫理やネット検索について解説した付録を充実させた。　　　　　　　　　　　　　　　◎1,000円

レポート・論文の書き方上級 改訂版

櫻井雅夫著　1998 年発行のロング＆ベストセラーの改訂版。定評のあった文献引用や、注の形式の類書を圧する充実した実例と解説に加え、具体例を一覧できる章を増補。大学院レベルでのスタンダードな参考書となっている。　　　　　　　　　　◎1,800円

思考を鍛えるレポート・論文作成法 第2版

井下千以子著　「書いては考える」のサイクルを意識できる、まったく新しいタイプのライティング指南書。大好評の初版をベースに構成とレイアウトを刷新し、ますます使いやすくなった第 2 版。初学者向けレポート・論文作成ガイドの決定版！　　◎1,200円

表示価格は刊行時の本体価格（税別）です。

慶應義塾大学出版会

アカデミック・スキルズ（第2版）
―大学生のための知的技法入門

佐藤望編著／湯川武・横山千晶・近藤明彦著　2006年の刊行以来、計4万部以上のロングセラーとなっている大学生向け学習指南書の決定版。様変わりした情報検索環境に対応した記述に変更し、より読みやすく章構成を再編。　◎1,000円

アカデミック・スキルズ
グループ学習入門―学びあう場づくりの技法

新井和広・坂倉杏介著　信頼できるグループの作り方、アイデアを引き出す技法、ITの活用法、ディベートの準備など、段階に合わせて、気をつけるポイントを紹介。　◎1,200円

アカデミック・スキルズ
データ収集・分析入門―社会を効果的に読み解く技法

西山敏樹・鈴木亮子・大西幸周著　モラルや道徳を守りながら、人や組織の行動を決定づけるデータを収集・分析し、考察や提案にまとめる手法を紹介。　◎1,800円

アカデミック・スキルズ
資料検索入門―レポート・論文を書くために

市古みどり編著・上岡真紀子・保坂睦著　テーマや考えを固めるために必要な資料（根拠や証拠）を検索し、入手するまでの「検索スキル」を身につけるための入門書。　◎1,200円

アカデミック・スキルズ
学生による学生のためのダメレポート脱出法

慶應義塾大学日吉キャンパス学習相談員著　実際に大学の学習相談に寄せられた質問を元に、レポート・論文執筆のポイントを、大学の学生相談員が「学生の目線」から易しく解説。◎1,200円

表示価格は刊行時の本体価格（税別）です。